THE PEACE DIVIDEND

A 75-year-old institution, **The Hindustan Times Group** is one of India's most respected media conglomerates. Publishers of the leading daily newspapers – the *Hindustan Times* in English and *Hindustan* in Hindi – their online edition, *Hindustantimes.com* is ranked by Forbes among the top ten newspaper websites in the world.

OTHER LOTUS TITLES:

HT Leadership Initiative	*India and the World: A Blueprint for Partnership and Growth*
HT Leadership Summit	*Building a Better Future*
HT Leadership Summit	*India: The Next Global Superpower?*
Aitzaz Ahsan	*The Indus Saga: The Making of Pakistan*
Alam Srinivas	*Storms in the Sea Wind: Ambani vs Ambani*
Amir Mir	*The True Face of Jehadis: Inside Pakistan's Terror Networks*
Bhawana Somaaya	*Hema Malini: The Authorized Biography*
Bidyut Chakrabarty	*Mahatma Gandhi: A Historical Biography*
Duff Hart-Davis	*Honorary Tiger: The Life of Billy Arjan Singh*
Frank Simoes	*Frank Unedited*
Frank Simoes	*Frank Simoes' Goa*
Joshua Key	*The Deserter's Tale*
L.S. Rathore	*The Regal Patriot: Maharaja Ganga Singh of Bikaner*
M.J. Akbar	*India: The Siege Within*
M.J. Akbar	*Kashmir: Behind the Vale*
M.J. Akbar	*Nehru: The Making of India*
M.J. Akbar	*Riot after Riot*
M.J. Akbar	*The Shade of Swords*
M.J. Akbar	*Byline*
M.J. Akbar	*Blood Brothers: A Family Saga*
Meghnad Desai	*Nehru's Hero Dilip Kumar: In the Life of India*
Nayantara Sahgal (ed.)	*Before Freedom: Nehru's Letters to His Sister*
Neesha Mirchandani	*Wisdom Song: The Life of Baba Amte*
Rohan Gunaratna	*Inside Al Qaeda*
Maj. Gen. Ian Cardozo	*Param Vir: Our Heroes in Battle*
Maj.Gen. Ian Cardozo	*The Sinking of INS Khukri: What Happened in 1971*
Maj. R.P. Singh, Kanwar Rajpal Singh	*Sawai Man Singh II of Jaipur: Life and Legend*
Mushirul Hasan	*India Partitioned. 2 Vols*
Mushirul Hasan	*John Company to the Republic*
Mushirul Hasan	*Knowledge, Power and Politics*
Rachel Dwyer	*Yash Chopra: Fifty Years of Indian Cinema*
Salma Ahmed	*Cutting Free: The Extraordinery Memoir of a Pakistani Woman*
Shrabani Basu	*Spy Princess: The Life of Noor Inayat Khan*
Thomas Weber	*Gandhi, Gandhism and the Gandhians*
V. Srinivasan	*New Age Management: Philosophy from Ancient Indian Wisdom*
Verghese Kurien, as told to Gouri Salvi	*I Too Had a Dream*
Vir Sanghvi	*Men of Steel: Indian Business Leaders in Candid Conversation*

FORTHCOMING TITLES:

Sharmistha Gooptu & Boria Majumdar (ed.)	*Revisiting 1857: Myth, Memory, History*
Shashi Joshi	*The Last Durbar*

THE PEACE DIVIDEND

Progress for India and South Asia

Hindustan Times LEADERSHIP initiative

"PEACE DIVIDEND" - PROGRESS FOR INDIA AND SOUTH ASIA

LOTUS COLLECTION

ROLI BOOKS

Lotus Collection

First published in hardback in 2004
This edition published in 2007
The Lotus Collection
An imprint of
Roli Books Pvt Ltd
M-75, G.K. II Market
New Delhi 110 048
Phones: ++91 (011) 2921 2271, 2921 2782
2921 0886, Fax: ++91 (011) 2921 7185
E-mail: roli@vsnl.com; Website: rolibooks.com

Also at
Varanasi, Bangalore, Jaipur and the Netherlands

Layout design: Narendra Shahi
Photo Credit: The Hindustan Times

ISBN: 978-81-7436-318-3
Rs. 250

Typeset in Photina MT by Roli Books Pvt Ltd
Printed at Tan Prints (India) Pvt. Ltd., Jhajjar, Haryana

THE PEACE DIVIDEND

Progress for India and South Asia

Hindustan Times
Leadership Initiative

Atal Bihari Vajpayee
Prime Minister of India

Mufti Mohammed Sayeed
Chief Minister of Jammu & Kashmir

Omar Abdullah
President, National Conference J & K

Sonia Gandhi
President, Congress Party & Leader of the Opposition

Lakshman Kadirgarmar
Adviser on International Affairs to the President of Sri Lanka

THE PEACE DIVIDEND

Progress for India and South Asia

Hindustan Times
Leadership Initiative

Asfandyar Wali Khan
President, Awami National Party, Pakistan

Benazir Bhutto
Former Prime Minister of Pakistan

Bimal Jalan
Member of Parliament & Former Governor, Reserve Bank of India

Manvinder Singh Banga
Chairman, Hindustan Lever Ltd.

Madeleine K. Albright
Former Secretary of State, US

ichard Haass
esident, Council on Foreign Relations

Francis Fukuyama
Prof. of International Political Economy, Johns Hopkins University.

.K. Singh
ember, Planning Commission of India

Anil D. Ambani
Vice-chairman, Reliance Industries Ltd.

hobhana Bharatiya
ice-chairperson of Hindustan Times

Hindustan Times
LEADERSHIP
initiative

"PEACE DIVIDEND" - PROGRESS FOR INDIA AND SOUTH ASIA

Keynote Address **97**
Benazir Bhutto 99
Q & A: Benazir Bhutto 109

Leveraging Peace for Profit **119**
Bimal Jalan 121
Nand Kishore Singh 125
Anil D.Ambani 129
Manvinder Singh Banga 135
Q & A: Leveraging Peace for Profit 141

Concluding Address **151**
Madeleine K. Albright 153
Q & A: Madeleine Albright 163

Glossary of Terms **172**

Profiles of Speakers

The Peace Dividend

Atal Bihari Vajpayee

Prime Minister of India

A long-time proponent of regional peace, Prime Minister Atal Bihari Vajpayee is today considered among the outstanding leaders and statesmen in the world. Vajpayee's key contribution goes beyond bringing a semblance of order to India—a tumultuous country in a tumultuous region—and overseeing its emergence as an economic and geopolitical force. Irrespective of the credits accruing from these initiatives, Vajpayee is likely to go down in history as a leader unafraid to talk peace with the country's most acrimonious neighbour, Pakistan, setting aside the intense provocation of war, territorial incursion and terrorism.

Vajpayee has led a case for India in the international arena that gathered momentum after 9/11, when India's long-stated position of being a victim of terrorism as state policy began to be appreciated. Alongside generating international support, Vajpayee kept up the pressure of peace on Pakistan and some of India's other neighbours with an effective policy of deterrence and détente.

Vajpayee's renewed overture of peace to Pakistan ahead of the Peace Dividend Conference, and his pioneering suggestions and vision of co-operation in security, open borders, and a common currency for South Asia at the conference have, by all available indications, paved the way for productive dialogue between India and Pakistan. This has the potential to transform South Asia.

Mufti Mohammad Sayeed

Chief Minister of Jammu & Kashmir

Mufti Mohammad Sayeed has since November 2002, with remarkable aplomb, headed a government in a state that is arguably the most contentious in recent history. Sayeed, a former home minister of India who later turned to politics in his home state of Jammu & Kashmir to found the People's Democratic Party, has since becoming chief minister, unveiled a controversial but increasingly accepted policy titled 'Healing Touch'.

This involves tackling endemic corruption in Jammu & Kashmir, and creating an environment to assimilate militants into civil society by offering amnesty, and creating more jobs and all-round development. This has not been easy, with terrorists keeping up the pressure, aided by political mentors. But the Mufti, who loves a game of bridge, may now see a few good hands of policy played out in the state, with the recent thaw in India-Pakistan relations, and the mood of dialogue among various pro-independence political factions in Jammu & Kashmir.

Omar Abdullah

President, National Conference

Often billed as a future chief minister of Jammu & Kashmir, Abdullah lost that race to Mufti Mohammad Sayeed in 2002. But the articulate and quick-thinking politician, a young-gun at 33, remains the head of one of the most powerful political dynasties in Jammu & Kashmir.

Abdullah's father Farooq was chief minister of Jammu & Kashmir through the most violent phases in the late 1980s and the 1990s. While his steadfast support of Indian policies during this time earned him a great degree of freedom to administer the state, the growth of vested interests and the electorate's increasing disenchantment with government cost the National Conference—and son and successor Omar—a chance to lead the state in 2002.

Omar remains an elected MP, and the president of the National Conference, the largest opposition party in the state. This foothold, combined with the modern thinking this former union minister of state for commerce and external affairs brings to the table, ensures Omar's place in the future dynamics of Jammu & Kashmir.

Sonia Gandhi

President, Congress Party,
and Leader of the Opposition

In the past five years, Sonia Gandhi has shed the tag of political amateur that her opponents—both outside and inside the Congress Party—ascribed to her. Equally, this former homemaker has led the Congress to the position of a vocal yet constructive opposition in Parliament, as elected MP and inheritor of the Nehru-Gandhi political legacy.

Long considered media shy and reclusive, Gandhi has over the past years become both more public and combative. She has impressed observers with her grasp of strategy. Gandhi's recent political plus-scores have been threefold. One is to lead a party in Parliament that is arguably the only one to offer solutions alongside criticism, the job of a true opposition party in the democratic mould. The second is her wisdom to allow coalition partner Mufti Mohammad Sayeed to form the government in Jammu & Kashmir, instead of staking a claim. And the third is a certificate of political maturity issued by her fiercest opponents in the BJP, who routinely say she is ineligible to be Prime Minister of India, as she was born an Italian.

Lakshman Kadirgamar

Adviser on International Affairs to the President of Sri Lanka; former Foreign Minister of Sri Lanka

As a lawyer, Lakshman Kadirgamar touched the pinnacle, becoming a President's Counsel. As a politician, he reached a height no other minority Tamil has, as a participant in the Sinhala-dominated, mainstream Sri Lankan politics. He became the country's first Tamil foreign minister.

As foreign minister, he did what most Sri Lankans thought was impossible: got the West—the US and UK—to ban the LTTE. And, few Sinhalese expected a Tamil to pursue this objective with such devotion and energy. While stressing the justifiability of the Tamil cause, Kadirgamar deprecated the separatism and militarism which had come to characterise the Tamil struggle for rights since the mid 1980s.

Currently, as international affairs advisor to President Chandrika Kumaratunga, Kadirgamar has been campaigning against separatism, militarism and what many feel is the tendency to compromise Sri Lanka's sovereignty and self-respect in an anxiety to find a quick solution to the ethnic question.

Asfandyar Wali Khan

President, Awami National Party, Pakistan

Asfandyar Wali Khan, grandson of 'Frontier Gandhi' Khan Abdul Ghaffar Khan, is scion of an illustrious political family of Pakistan that played a major role in India's freedom struggle. Currently the president of the Awami National Party, he has served as a member of the North West Frontier Province Assembly, and the two Houses of Pakistan's Parliament.

An MBA, Asfandyar Wali was elected to the Pakistan Parliament's Upper House, the Senate, in February 2003. In the North West Frontier Province, the ANP confronts a provincial government led by the Mutahida Majlis-e-Ammal, a right wing alliance of religio-political parties with deep anti-US, pro-jehadi leanings. But the ANP has persisted with its national aspirations and universal principles. Its leaders see it as a "bulwark against extremism and fundamentalism." Towards that end, the ANP had opposed Taliban rule in Afghanistan.

In the post-9/11 phase, the ANP spoke up for liberal, democratic and secular values, holding public meetings against the Taliban. Having endorsed the 'liberation' of Afghanistan, Asfandyar Wali recently led an ANP delegation to that country.

Richard Haass

President, Council on Foreign Relations, New York

It is a measure of his eminent reputation that when Richard Haass left the State Department as Secretary of State Colin Powell's principal advisor in 2003, he was made head of the US's most influential foreign policy think-tank, the Council on Foreign Relations.

There is almost no international hotspot Haass has not dabbled in, from keeping a lid on the Balkan powder keg, Northern Ireland's conflict, setting rules for intervening in Rwanda, preparing blueprints for the rebuilding of Afghanistan and, of course, trying to ensure India and Pakistan talk rather than fight. The author of nine books on foreign policy and one on public sector management (his opening bit of advice: being intelligent can be a drawback when it comes to getting things done in government), Haass is no peacenik. But he is a quintessential problem-solver who knows the world is complex, policy a labyrinth, and power finite.

Haass has strongly and forcefully argued that a pillar of US grand strategy must be to inject democracy into the Muslim world. He is forthright in saying the US is partly to blame for the ballot box deficit among Arabs. But he has no doubts this is the long-term vaccine against Al Qaeda, and has stressed on America's support for democratic processes elsewhere in the world.

Francis Fukuyama

Professor of International Political Economy at the Paul H. Nitze School of Advanced International Studies, Johns Hopkins University

Twenty years ago, Fukuyama was just another brilliant Beltway diplomat and analyst. He worked in the RAND Corporation. He then held key positions in the US State Department, and was a delegate at the Camp David peace process in 1981-82.

In 1992, he wrote *The End of History*. His title simply meant that with the collapse of communism, there were no longer any viable alternatives to democratic capitalism. It proved a beacon in a world bewildered at the sudden end of the Cold War. Fukuyama's latest book is titled *Our Postmodern Future*.

Behind all these phrases is a running theme. Namely, that the broad current of history has shown that democracy and the market are the best principles to organise a society. Yes, there will be problems and setbacks. But modernity always wins, and events like 9/11 are only 'serious detours'.

Fukuyama is a warrior of ideas. He looked at the disruptive effect of the information revolution. Conclusion: The social order will rebuild itself. In his last work, Fukuyama looked at biotechnology and what it meant for liberal society, because it provided "new opportunities for the political control of behaviour". He still sees this as a greater concern than Islamic suicide bombers.

Benazir Bhutto

Former Prime Minister of Pakistan

To be elected prime minister of a country as volatile as Pakistan is a difficult task. Benazir Bhutto ruled Pakistan for nearly nine years, as the first woman to head the government of an Islamic state.

She has spent seven years either in jail or in exile, for political reasons. Her worst run-ins have been with Pakistan's all-powerful military leaders. One of them, Zia ul Haq, hanged her father. The military helped stage a constitutional coup against her in 1996. General Pervez Musharraf, Pakistan's present dictator, holds her husband in jail and keeps Bhutto in de facto exile. Despite this, Bhutto remains an outspoken critic of Musharraf. She calls the Kargil war "the biggest blunder committed in the history of Pakistan."

As prime minister, Bhutto was responsible both for reaching out to India with a peace overture, as she was later of acquiescing to increase militancy as a tactical weapon in Jammu & Kashmir. After 9/11, Bhutto, and the Pakistan People's Party that she leads from exile, have reoriented themselves, and Bhutto is presently among the most vocal members of a group that cautions India of the dangers of trying to come to peace with a military dictator.

Bimal Jalan

MP; Former Governor, Reserve Bank of India

Bimal Jalan knows numbers like few others in India. When he was finance secretary during the Gulf War shock of 1990-91, India's foreign exchange reserves were scraping the barrel. When he demitted office as governor of the Reserve Bank more than a decade later in September 2003, India's foreign exchange reserves were inching close to $100 billion, among the highest in the world, and the country's monetary policies were being lauded globally. Jalan's nomination to the Upper House of Parliament was for a job well done.

But Jalan has done more than just witnessed—and helped bridge—the gap between low and high. He is among a handful of eminently qualified academicians and theoreticians in India, who successfully transitioned from theory to practice. Educated at Calcutta, Cambridge and Oxford Universities, Jalan moved smoothly from academia and research with India's top economic and policy think tanks, to government. He was chief economic advisor to the Government of India; banking secretary; finance secretary; member-secretary of the Planning Commission; and chairman of the Economic Advisory Council to the Prime Minister of India.

Jalan has served and represented India on the executive boards of the World Bank and the International Monetary Fund. And, during the East Asian contagion of 1997, successfully managed the impact as governor of the Reserve Bank. Bureaucrat-banker and wry wit, Jalan is a leading expert on inflation, interest rate regimes and policy.

Nand Kishore Singh

Member, Planning Commission of India

N.K. Singh is known for his pro-reform imperatives and has, in various capacities, been a key constituent of the core group of economic decision makers in the past decade. Notably, while working as secretary to the prime minister, Singh acted as Atal Bihari Vajpayee's main advisor on economic issues. He was member-secretary of the Prime Minister's Council on trade and industry, as well as the Economic Advisory Council.

Apart from his responsibilities in the Planning Commission, 'Nandu' Singh is the chairman of the steering group on foreign direct investment as well as the steering group on energy and transport policy. He also heads the group on financial resources and management, apart from the inter-ministerial group on tax policy.

Singh has also been revenue secretary in the Ministry of Finance. He was responsible for human resource development, administration and collection of revenues of the Central Government. Singh played a key role in the preparation of the Union Budget, particularly the Revenue Budget including taxation proposals and tax reform policy. He was associated with investigation and enforcement of tax frauds, money-laundering and narcotic offences.

Anil D.Ambani

Vice-chairman, Reliance Industries Limited

Anil Ambani is known as much for being a fitness freak and distance runner, as the catalyst of some of the finest deals in Indian finance. Over the years he has helped Reliance Industries grow into India's biggest private sector conglomerate with key interests in petrochemicals, energy, telecommunications and biotechnology.

A graduate of the Wharton Business School, Ambani, 46, holds the post of vice chairman and managing director of Reliance Industries. He spearheads the group's energy ventures as chairman and managing director of Reliance Energy Limited. Ambani has pioneered many financial innovations in the Indian capital markets, and led India's first forays into global capital markets with international offerings of global depository receipts and convertibles, including the issue of the first 100-year Yankee bond from an Asian corporation.

Ambani, a prime mover of national and regional energy security issues, is a member of the Wharton Board of Overseers, University of Pennsylvania. The Central Electricity Regulatory Commission in July 2003 appointed him Member of the Central Advisory Committee. Earlier in May 2003, Government of India nominated him Chairman of the Board of Governors of the National Safety Council. In January 2003, the Government of India nominated him Member of the Board of Governors, Indian Institute of Management, Ahmedabad.

Manvinder Singh Banga

Chairman, Hindustan Lever Limited

Popularly known as Vindi, at 48 Manvinder Singh Banga is the chairman of India's largest FMCG group and holds the responsibility for Unilever's businesses in South Asia, a region he knows intimately. Hindustan Lever has for long been a motivating force in promoting business ties in the region, and Vindi continues to champion the cause of cross-border investment for reasons many policymakers tend to overlook: increasing efficiencies and profit alongside generating employment and trust.

A distinguished alumnus of two premier institutions of India, the Indian Institute of Technology, Delhi and Indian Institute of Management, Ahmedabad, Vindi has spent his entire career at

Hindustan Lever, with a stint at Unilever headquarters in London, where was a senior vice president in 1998.

On the board and managing committees of many trade and non-trade institutions, including the Indian School of Business, Hyderabad, and the Indian Institute of Management, Ahmedabad, he is an independent director on the board of Maruti Udyog, India's largest automobile manufacturer. Vindi is also a member of the India Aids Initiative Programme Board.

Madeleine K. Albright

Former Secretary of State, United States of America

She is a stalwart of the Democratic Party and a lifelong liberal. But, Madeleine Albright is no pushover. As secretary of state during Bill Clinton's presidency, she accused the Pentagon of being gun-shy, and famously ticked off Fidel Castro. More recently, she has stated that George W. Bush's foreign policy "is not good for America, not good for the world."

She is a proponent of the institution of the United Nations. During the Clinton administration, Albright maintained a savage sanctions policy peppered with missiles, against Saddam Hussein's regime. But she gives a thumbs-down to the present invasion, saying the US should have concentrated on Afghanistan.

Albright is equally unflinching in her views on South Asia, a region she knows well and continues to take a keen interest in. Her father, Joseph Korbel was a leading expert on the region, in particular, on Kashmir. During the Clinton presidency, Albright was at the forefront of managing the US thaw with India. She was responsible for the driving policy during the tricky phase in 1998-99—two years that saw nuclear testing in the subcontinent and the war in Kargil.

Foreword

Shobhana Bhartia

Vice-chairperson Hindustan Times

We believe that a serious newspaper must do more than just mere reportage or carry interesting articles. A great newspaper is one that defines its role in terms of contributing to intellectual debate and shaping the future.

The *Hindustan Times* Leadership Initiative is part of that endeavour. We hope to gather the best and the brightest and to provide a platform for the free and candid exchange of ideas. We are pleased that at our first conference, we have been able to bring together some of the most influential, thoughtful and incisive minds, not just in this region, but in the world. And we hope that the ideas that flow out of this room over the next two days will contribute towards providing a blueprint for action and will help determine the agenda for the future.

When we planned the Leadership Initiative, I was particularly keen that the first conference should focus on peace and prosperity in South Asia. Some of the reasons for this are obvious. We do, after all, live in South Asia.

But there are other, less immediately obvious, reasons as well. For a start, I do not think we can achieve global prosperity or world peace unless the issues confronting South Asia are suitably addressed.

This region is home to one quarter of humanity. By the year 2050, this figure will rise to one-third of the world's population. Even before that happens, a full quarter of the world's economic output will come from South Asia. The region will not just be one of the world's greatest markets; it will also be one of the world's great production centres.

In many ways, South Asia is a microcosm of the rest of the world. It is home to nearly all of the world's great religions: Hinduism, Islam, Christianity and Buddhism, among others.

In this region we also find conflicts whose resolution will determine the future of our world. The conflicts between old and new;

between religious fundamentalism and modernity; between terrorism and civilisation; between military dictatorships and civilian rule; between authoritarianism and liberalism; and between ethnicity and nationhood.

If the conflicts that bedevil South Asia are not resolved, the fall-out will shake the whole world. We all recognise how a single nuclear conflict will change the shape of modern warfare. And we have seen how a single spark in a small part of South Asia can lead to terrorist movements that threaten the stability of all modern civilisations.

In today's global environment, events in one part of the world can have consequences that are felt thousands of miles away. For many years, the international community ignored Afghanistan and watched silently as the Taliban destroyed the Bamiyan Buddhas, persecuted women and minorities, and unleashed a reign of terror on the people

We see peace as more than just the necessary precondition for stability

of Afghanistan. *That* silence and *that* neglect were to have terrible consequences, which the world recognised only when two planes hit the World Trade Centre in faraway New York.

That pattern is repeated week after week, month after month. A terrorist movement run by an Arab, headquartered in Afghanistan and targeting the United States, can strike at will anywhere in the world. And the victims could be of any nationality.

That is how interlinked the world is today. We ignore unrest, discontentment or oppression anywhere in the world at our peril. The consequences of such neglect can explode in our own backyards.

In the long run, if there is no peace in South Asia, there can be no peace in the whole world. If there is no economic progress in South Asia, then the instability and frustration that results from the misery of millions of people will shake the foundations of international order and stability.

Hence, the theme for this conference. South Asia matters. And that's not just because we are meeting in Delhi. But because whatever happens in this region, can have a profound impact on the rest of the world.

We have called this conference the Peace Dividend. There is a reason for that. We see peace as more than just the absence of conflict. We see it as a necessary precondition for stability and prosperity.

Whatever the problems within our region, there is no doubt that it is also home to millions of massively talented and skilled individuals. Wherever in the world you go, you will find people from South Asia. In such fields as information technology, we are among the global leaders. But there are many other areas where South Asians have excelled and have competed with the best in the world.

That, in a sense, is the paradox of South Asia. How do we unleash the innate talent of our people within our own countries? How do we create an environment that allows them to excel and prosper at home just as much as they do when they go abroad?

The answer, I believe, lies in peace and in the resolution of conflict. Prosperity is the greatest dividend from peace. Create an environment that is safe, secure and stable and we will unleash the genius of the South Asian people.

Over the next two days, we will have the privilege of listening to leaders in public life, in business, in the field of ideas and in the areas

absence of conflict. We see it as a and prosperity.

of academics. We will question them, discuss the issues with them and try and find some answers.

Our role, as befits a paper such as the *Hindustan Times*, is to bring the best and the brightest together.

On the subject of peace and the dividends it brings, there can be no speaker whose credentials are more appropriate than Shri Atal Bihari Vajpayee.

As prime minister, he has constantly and continuously put his reputation and his career on the line in his quest for a peaceful South Asia. He has spoken often of the need for understanding and for dialogue. And he has recognised that all progress is, ultimately, predicated on peace.

This conference represents our attempt to understand the conflicts that trouble our region. It is an effort to help resolve such conflicts, to create greater understanding and to sketch out a roadmap for the way forward.

Inaugural Address

Atal Bihari Vajpayee

'No one thought Apartheid South Africa could be transformed bloodlessly into Mandela's Rainbow Country ... Not many would have predicted that the hostile suspicion between Russia and China could be converted into a strategic partnership ... In today's context, collective regional interest is an expression of enlightened self-interest.'

Atal Bihari Vajpayee

Prime Minister of India

When the *Hindustan Times* Leadership Initiative invited me to this conference, what really attracted me was the powerful imagery of the peace dividend as the engine of progress in our region. At the same time, I must confess with some sadness that, over half a century after all the countries of our region attained independence, this truth still needs to be emphasised.

The peace dividend for South Asia is the creation of new hope and opportunity for its billion and a half people. We need no stronger justification for peace than this simple statement. The investment inputs required to reap this dividend are pragmatic politics, rational economics and popular participation.

There can be no argument about our inherent advantages, common interests and complementary strengths, which present a tremendous opportunity for our region to realise its full potential:

- First and foremost, our rich and varied human resources. Our citizens have created waves around the world with their technical, financial and managerial expertise. Their energies and talents can find greater application in regional cooperative enterprises.
- Second, our populations are younger than the world average, and will therefore constitute an increasing proportion of the global workforce in the future.
- Third, our technological advances have put us at the vanguard of today's Knowledge Economy, enabling us to accelerate our development process.

- Fourth, the size and increasing purchasing power of our collective markets create economies of scale for cost-effective production.
- Fifth, efficient exploitation of our synergies can vastly enhance intra-regional trade, even as we work towards a rule-based international trading regime.
- Sixth, the region has massive untapped capabilities for hydropower and unexploited hydrocarbons, which can more than meet its huge energy deficit.
- Seventh, the rich diversity of our bio-resources—in the Himalayan region and elsewhere—are yet to be exploited for our common benefit.
- Eighth, our combined political weight and economic strength can give us considerable leverage in pursuing our shared objective for a cooperative multi-polar world order.

The peace dividend lies in converting this exciting potential into vibrant reality. Our region is heir to centuries-old traditions of tolerance, pluralism and creative interaction. We need to recapture this ethos in the modern context.

In the post-Cold War world of globalisation, countries around the world are increasingly focusing on regional economics. Political disputes have been resolved diplomatically or quietly deferred for tackling at a more opportune time. Conflict has given way to cooperation; dialogue moderates differences. There is a clear recognition that hostility only stunts economies, inhibits trade and retards progress.

This realisation has dawned not only in the developed world, but also in developing regions that have experienced bitter differences and violent conflicts in the past. It encompasses Mercosur and the Andean Pact, COMESA and SADC, NAFTA and APEC. Nearer home, we have the outstanding example of ASEAN. South Asia needs the wisdom to heed these lessons.

By most estimates trade within regions accounts for nearly three-fourths of global trade. Yet, inspite of our geographical proximity, shared economic characteristics and similar development infrastructure intra-South Asia trade is under 5 per cent of our total foreign trade.

We must discard the myth that, because of the asymmetries in our economies, the smaller countries do not benefit from closer economic integration within South Asia. Our free trade agreements with Nepal and Sri Lanka have resulted in narrowing the trade deficit of both these countries with India. In fact, the success of the India-Sri Lanka Free Trade Agreement has inspired us to expand its scope to cover services and investment in a comprehensive economic partnership agreement.

Energy is one area with the greatest promise of mutually enriching partnerships. Nepal and Bhutan today have an estimated potential of 100,000 mw of environmentally clean hydropower. Bangladesh has similarly promising reserves of natural gas. They need to sell these energy sources. India is the only viable buyer and its energy demands are expanding exponentially. There is obvious scope for win-win arrangements. The hydroelectric projects in Bhutan illustrate this dramatically. Bhutan's per capita income of US$600 today is expected to double by the end of 2005, when the 1,020 Megawatt Tala power plant is completed.

The optimum management of our regional water resources for irrigation, navigation and flood control can have a multiplier effect on infrastructure, development and growth in our entire region. This requires not only financial investments, but also maturity of policy. We should recognise that an enduring partnership can only be built on the basis of each country wisely exercising the rights of a lower riparian, and responsibly fulfilling the obligations of an upper riparian.

Our region sits astride the land routes and sea-lanes that connect the world's big energy sources of the Middle East to the expanding energy markets of East and Southeast Asia. With our extended neighbourhood of Iran and Afghanistan, our land mass also links the new energy sources of Central Asia with the warm water ports of the Indian Ocean in the south. It does not require much imagination to envisage how close regional cooperation can cash in on the strategic importance of our location.

Our most important common war today is against poverty, disease, hunger and underdevelopment. We can share experiences and promote intra-regional linkages for economic and social development. A small but significant beginning has been made by our SAARC Experts Group on Poverty

 Alleviation. The group, drawn from all SAARC countries, has extensively documented the best practices in poverty alleviation programmes across the region. It has made detailed recommendations for regional dissemination of information on these practices and for regional capacity building. We have to show dedication in implementation of these recommendations and multiply such examples of regional experience sharing.

As we develop greater economic stakes in each other, we can put aside mistrust and dispel unwarranted suspicions. We will also develop mutual sensitivity to each others' concerns and promote more of our common interests. If we provide legitimate avenues of free commercial interaction, we can eradicate the black market and underground trade. We could jointly tackle smuggling, drug trafficking, money laundering and other trans-national crimes, which today flourish in our region because of our mutual rivalries and inadequate coordination. Once we reach that stage, we would not be far from mutual security cooperation, open borders and even a single currency.

If this seems unrealistic and Utopian, perhaps we are being unnecessarily cynical. Let us remember that the world did not anticipate the sudden end to the Cold War, or the collapse of the Berlin Wall. No one thought Apartheid South Africa could be transformed bloodlessly into Mandela's Rainbow Country. Not many political analysts would have predicted that the hostile suspicion between Russia and China could be converted in such a short time into a strategic partnership.

Each one of these developments flowed from objective factors in the global environment, but actually occurred because of some enlightened and responsible decisions by people at the helm of affairs.

I would suggest that the demands of globalisation and the aspirations of our people provide the objective bases for our energetic pursuit of a harmoniously integrated South Asia. Our people, businesses and organisations are waiting to interact more closely with each other. This includes producers and consumers, investors and markets, doctors and patients, artists and audiences, students and universities. They are all part of the supply and demand dynamics of a vast subcontinent. They see the unexploited potential in their own neighbourhood. They have waited for over a half-century for its fulfillment and are now impatient to move ahead.

We can sense this impatience in the outpouring of popular sentiment after our initiatives. The increased travel between India and Pakistan of parliamentarians, businessmen, artists and sportsmen shows the intense desire for amity and goodwill. We have to respond to this desire by seeking every possible way to banish hostility and promote peace.

If we in South Asia look back objectively at the experiences of our freedom struggles and of our nation-building, the one stark lesson that stands out is the imperative of forging a unity based on our commonalities. Whenever we have dissipated our energies in internal squabbling, external forces have come in to sort out our differences and stayed on to exploit our resources. We should never create the possibility of reliving these historical experiences in new forms and on different fronts.

All these are aspects which we could discuss as we exchange ideas on the economic, strategic and geopolitical future of India and South Asia, ahead of the forthcoming SAARC Summit. Our search for pragmatism, maturity and wisdom will have to involve both governments and civil society. It will also require a widespread understanding that in today's context, collective regional interest is an expression of enlightened self-interest.

The **Kashmir Tangle**
IS THERE A WAY OUT?

Mufti Mohammad Sayeed
Omar Abdullah

‘The people of Muslim countries need to introspect why Islam has got a bad name. Such a review is routinely overlooked in the West where traditional orientalism maintains its hegemony, and overriding the dynamics of cultures and the diversity of what is within them ... There are serious movements of self-assessment taking place within Islam.’

Mufti Mohammad Sayeed

Chief Minister, Jammu & Kashmir

Given my current position and, may I say, my preoccupation, I will take you through a small slice of world history. Small, but very intense and very troubled, one that has engaged my peers and greater leaders—the issue of Jammu and Kashmir.

Let me start by saying that any attempt to place the Kashmir issue into water-tight compartments—Islamic militancy, cross border terrorism, secessionist urgency, ethno-national demand—does less good and more damage to the variety of factors, and the sheer complexity of elements and the radical hybridity that have caused the problem in Kashmir. It is a highly volatile and extremely contentious matter for which there are no—indeed, cannot be—any easy answers. Roadmaps prejudge the issue; readymade solutions make the problem a distorted image of what it actually is; and models make a mockery of specificity of the issue.

All that one can hope to discuss at a forum like this is to look for a framework for a solution, a context in which the issue can be placed and a contour of solutions worked out. Prior to doing so, it might help if we quickly run through the major strands of thought in the resolution paradigm.

First and perhaps the oldest are the 'internationalists' who look towards the United Nations for a settlement. I believe that it is time we look beyond it. Sometimes those who are aggrieved use the international community as an object for appeal for more than human rights. But the fact is, there is no international community.

I believe there was some type of structure as long as the United Nations was an organisation. With the United Nations having been marginalised, there is no Centre where the long-term view can be taken, and a platform of principle constructed. If we go to the United Nations now, it is akin to assuming the position of litigant before a court that does not exist.

The second most popular strand of thought comes from the 'status quoists'. They want to convert the Line of Control in Jammu and Kashmir into an international border. Given that it is the line of conflict, to recommend that the problem can be resolved on the basis of the Line of Control can at best be a part of the solution, not a stand-alone solution. Internal dimensions of the problem cannot be wished away.

The oft-repeated demand for autonomy, which has its origin in the early 1950s is itself a compromise solution. Even though it recognises the ethno-nationalism of Kashmiris, the implied political position is that ethnicity need not engender nationhood. That is why independence is not the pursued goal of the autonomist viewpoint.

Instead, the issue was whether Kashmir should join Pakistan or India. The political movement of the mainstream parties was not to pursue the process of nationality-formation to the point where political structures were sought to be made congruent with nationality by creating an independent entity. This came to the fore in 1975. The view thereafter was that even if the Kashmiris are a distinct nationality, it does not axiomatically follow that they are entitled to a nation-state—hence, the desire to create an enclave of autonomy within India.

While most political analysts subscribing to the autonomist viewpoint do recognise the ethno-nationalism of the Kashmiris—*Kashmiriyat*—they differ from the advocates of independence. They go further, and make an ethno-territorial demand.

Further, the basis of this form of autonomy as practiced in the early 1950s was flawed, as it sought to create an enclave of federalism within a unitary system, and combine the advantages of a loose federation with those of a centralised system, without impairing its functioning.

But now, the situation has changed with regional parties gaining prominence and the Centre being ruled by a coalition of parties. Even though it is the same constitution, the spirit is far more federal today and the autonomy issue may not suffer from the same ills as it did earlier. A fact nobody could have foreseen is this development of regional aspirations and regional forces coming to the fore. Symbolising regional aspirations while maintaining commitment to the national integrity or unity of the nation are the states of Andhra Pradesh, West Bengal, Tamil-nadu, and North-east.

Therefore, India is not written in our constitution. Our constitution is unitary as well as federal, but the federal structure of the country does get strengthened. The way the chief ministers of Andhra Pradesh and Karnataka deal with multinationals could be compared to the United States of America. Their states have the residuary powers but here, a truly Indian federal structure is present.

I must say, if Mohammad Ali Jinnah, the founder of the two-nation theory, were alive to see the flowering of Indian federalism and democracy, I don't think he would have insisted on an independent state. He was more for decentralisation of the country, for more federalism. So it augurs well for our country. Regional parties symbolising regional aspirations is a totally federal structure.

How can one conceive of political autonomy without a fiscal autonomy? Political autonomy derives its substance and sustainability from economic independence.

The most serious problem with the lobby opposing the pre-1953 status is that then there would be no financial links between the Union of India and the state of Jammu and Kashmir. In the current dispensation it will be difficult for the State government even to pay its wage bill, let alone finance its development. This is not the reflection of unviability of the state economy, but a commentary on how over the years, successive regimes—at the Centre and the State—colluded and worked in tandem to make a vibrant economy completely dependent on central resource transfers. In its present form, this demand shows a complete stagnation of ideas and lack of foresight. Kashmir has the great potential of generating power but owing to a lack of resources we are not able to benefit from this situation. So in a way, a greater fiscal autonomy is a greater priority for people of Jammu and Kashmir.

The real danger in this case is that the autonomist viewpoint can be very easily diluted, which then goes to compromise the basic principles of ethno-nationalism. The entire effort to create an autonomous unit in recognition of historically inherited ethno-nationalism can, with the stroke of a pen be firmly condemned to a Byzantine labyrinth of Indian federal issues. Indeed, in the 1950s, the position of the Head of State—Prime Minister of Jammu and Kashmir—was not institutionalised, and therefore could be subverted without much effort.

The important point is not to look for solutions in the past, but to find them in the future. A return to the past may not be possible—indeed, it may not even be desirable. The world has undergone a change and we have to be a part of that changed system. The past offers no hope.

It is very important to recognise that we are living through a period where definitions of cultures, societies, sovereignty, and nationality are changing very rapidly and radically. All these issues have gone through a large number of transformations and sometimes, dramatic shifts.

Along with the end of political bi-polarity, an equally important set of factors has been the pressures and opportunities of globalisation. Technological innovations in communication and transportation, and in particular, the movement of capital across borders, have circumvented or eroded traditional state sovereignty not only in the conduct of international finance and trade, but increasingly, in their own domestic affairs. This is a crucial fact that will have to be borne in mind for any future dispensation that we might conceive for Jammu and Kashmir.

The vacuum left behind after the Cold War, coupled with the vagaries of globalisation has created serious external strains on the traditional nation-state apparatus, particularly in the developing world. Many developing states that were already weakened or failing due to a variety of internal factors will be under greater pressure now. All this will lead to newer and more relevant definitions of sovereignty.

Indeed, I think that the seeds of a solution lie in using the logic of this change that is spearheaded by globalisation to evolve a framework for new political dispensation in Jammu and Kashmir. This will resolve the issue on a long-term basis. In this context, our first move has to be to look for a SAARC economic space where we can have a free movement of factors of production like labour and capital; greater market relations; a single currency; consistent and congruous monetary and fiscal policy; and a uniform trade policy.

Today, the principle idea in the global order is that economic interests override all other kinds of interest. It is believed that with binding and self-propelling economic interests, political disputes will automatically become less intense, frozen positions will surely get thawed, and all economic relations will bring us to being just one step away from political resolutions.

Fortunately, we are thinking along these lines at a time when in the Islamic world there is an extraordinarily energetic debate taking place, from Morocco to Indonesia, about what Islam actually is after the 9/11 attacks on the World Trade Centre. The image of Islam has been damaged in a very bad way. The concept of Islam, the message of Islam, has not been conveyed properly. Therefore there is in-depth introspection among Muslims. Even some fringe elements have adopted terrorist activities.

This is not the whole Islamic message. Violence is only from the fringe elements. They should be isolated. They should be condemned. *That* is the message.

Muslim countries need to introspect why Islam has got a bad name. Such a review is routinely overlooked in the West where traditional orientalism maintains its hegemony, overriding the dynamic of cultures and the diversity of what is within them.

All this will have a bearing on how the masses in Kashmir react to a solution, how they see the road ahead, and how actively they further it. It is no longer correct to say that, globally Islam is in the grip of a wave of unyielding fundamentalism. This is very far from the truth. There are serious movements of self-assessment taking place within Islam.

Finally, I think it is of utmost importance to recognise the dimension of the problem.

The first generation, which was involved in the country's freedom movement, did not accept divides on the basis of religion but across secular lines. We projected our *Kashmiriyat*, we projected our secular fabric, we thought we would make

Kashmir a showcase. It was the vision of Jawaharlal Nehru and Sheikh Mohammad Abdullah to make Kashmir a showcase of how Muslims, Hindus and other religions in different regions can survive with unity in diversity. But, because of us politicians, this experiment did not succeed.

Although the first generation did not accept a division of Kashmir on the basis of religion, the Hindu-Muslim issue did become a part of the mental makeup. The second generation who witnessed the 1965 war between India and Pakistan and the East Pakistan crisis in 1971, responded differently. And, a majority of them developed animosity, mistrust and suspicion towards each other. Using nationalistic perspectives, this generation was not prepared to maintain friendly relations with each other.

As historical memories recede, the third generation, in their thirties, or slightly more, is not emotionally swayed like the earlier generations were. This third generation did not witness any large-scale war between our country and Pakistan. Emotional detachment helped them to rise above psychological barriers and be more forward-looking and future- oriented.

As Stephen Cohen puts it, “A third generation is now emerging. This third generation does not have a sense of responsibility for gloomy history. Their competence and their interest in the things that matter, a fresh approach to economic issues, plus the collapse of many institutions dominated by past generations will bring them to power—sooner than later. More than any other development in the region, this new group of regional leaders will make it possible for change to occur.”

A generational shift in the politics of Kashmir is nearing completion. This process is well and truly entrenched. Look around, and you will find that every major political group in the wide spectrum of the state has as its leader, a person in his or her forties, or less. Moulvi Omar Farooq, Sajjad and Bilal Lone, Omar Abdullah, Mohammad Yasin Malik, Shabbir Shah, and of course, the leader of my party, Mehbooba Mufti, are all examples.

To see such a confluence of young blood and brains across all shades of the political spectrum is rare indeed. Not many places in the world can claim to have a top political leadership in its late twenties and early thirties. I can’t think of any other such place, especially in the age-obsessed politics of the subcontinent. That this then should happen in Kashmir, the oldest and the most intractable problem in the world I believe, not only augurs well but makes the static state of affairs interestingly significant and pregnant with possibilities. A breakthrough is more than a mere possibility when the excess baggage of the past is not a hindrance.

Will the new generation bring about the minimisation of ethnic, class, regional and ideological distinctions that have independently and collectively a major bearing on the core of the Kashmir issue? Or will it heighten these tensions? One hopes not. However, one does hope that there is a complete break from the past in the manner in which the issue is conceptualised, and the politics conducted. Unfortunately, my generation has let the issue fester. We are guilty, and shall be deemed so in the court of history, unless we act—and act fast.

There will certainly be an attitudinal change. The young the world over are increasingly connected to international culture through new means of mass communication. Slow economic development and limited political opportunities threaten governmental legitimacy all over the globe. But moves towards democratisation *are* taking place at many levels.

To understand these disparate and interconnected dynamics, and initiate action, what the new leadership—irrespective of political affiliations and goals—needs to do is combine comparative politics and political economy with emerging international political order and static analysis.

What have we achieved? To start with, we have shown that political fundamentalism is the race of frustration, which takes root due to a lack of dialogue. It is not the norm, but exception, to the historically known mental makeup of Kashmiris.

In the first year of governance we did not focus our attention so much on changing the political system. But we tried to change the structures in which political, civil and economic life is conducted. Our attention went to the major responsibilities of state, which include provision of public goods, and providing the infrastructure to allow for economic activity.

This is a part of my overall resolution strategy, because I do believe that complex political emergencies are not only to be found in the issues around which conflicts are politicised, such as ethnicity or regional identity but also in the basic failure of governance. In fact, it is often this failure that is the cause for politicisation of ethnic identity issues. So, we have tried to focus on these less glamorous issues of conflict resolution in the first year.

It must be recognised that, for the first time in the troubled history of our state, the State Government is not in an adversarial role. Talks are being conducted with separatist groups—indeed, we are the facilitators, and see this as a major achievement of one year in power.

We believe that we have met our first objective of being a means for effective articulation of political, social and economic aspirations of the Kashmiris. The illegitimate symbiotic relationship with the state and its repressive measures and civil bureaucracy, which had imparted an authoritarian stand to governance in Jammu and Kashmir has been substantially broken. This has allowed us to pursue a meaningful non-violent agenda.

We have also stopped the marginalisation of moderates in the political spectrum of Kashmir. It cannot be denied that, to a large extent, this has been possible because of a change in the attitudes and policies of the Government of India. The grim message of a central authority determined to use coercion over an increasingly alienated people was the source of this marginalisation. This then has decisively undergone a change.

We are now at the threshold of our third step: empowering the legitimate democratic institutions of the state to the extent that they are not manipulated by anyone. For instance, if the current or future legislature of the state that has been democratically elected makes recommendations that are within the purview of the constitution of the state and the county, it is obligatory on the part of the Centre to seriously consider the proposals.

Nothing shows the change in this attitude more clearly than the recent state elections. Instead of raking up bitterness of the past and raising the ante with Pakistan, the attitude of the entire campaign in the recent elections was quite the contrary. We warmed up to Pakistan; we focused on progress, not parochialism; we discussed development; and initiated dialogue. Nothing can be more heartening than that. As we sit here in the middle of a Delhi winter I smell spring in the political climate of the sub-continent. The blossoms are not far! And as you all know,the blossoms in Kashmir are the best in the world.

‘The fact is that you cannot question a peace dividend for the people of Jammu and Kashmir. What we need to do is try and reinforce this belief in our neighbour. We need to let Pakistan understand that there is a peace dividend for Pakistan as well.’

Omar Abdullah

President, National Conference,
Jammu & Kashmir

I am usually very nervous when I talk about Jammu and Kashmir, for a number of reasons. I look forward to talking about a subject that is dearest to my heart. And then I stand up on the stage and realise that it is not a subject I can be dispassionate or academic about. This subject at times overwhelms me, when I realise that what we are living through is what we in Jammu and Kashmir have lived through. I look at the present, and the hope and expectations that prevails for the future. And how many times in the past, from 1947 onwards, and most certainly from 1989-1990 onwards, our hopes have been dashed, and how many times we have had our expectations raised to new levels just to have them brought down to previously unfelt depths. It was extremely brave on the part of the *Hindustan Times* to put both me and the chief minister on the same stage. In Jammu and Kashmir we are hardcore political rivals.

Listening to the chief minister's opening remarks, wherein he very eloquently tore apart two of my father's (former Chief Minister, Farooq Abdullah) often stated positions on solutions to Jammu and Kashmir, namely, greater autonomy to Jammu and Kashmir, and the conversion of the Line of Control into the border, I can't help but imagine that some clever speech writers have done a diplomatic job at ripping apart the National Conference's position without making it appear that he was taking a very strong political line.

We have never maintained that the conversion of the Line of Control, or even, the restoration of greater autonomy, is the only solution to Jammu and Kashmir. There can be no one who can say, 'I have the best solution for Jammu and Kashmir and this is the only one that is applicable.' Because, if there was an individual of that nature, or if there was a solution like that, the person would have been bestowed with a Nobel Peace Prize and would have been a great hero in India, and perhaps, in Pakistan as well. But, there is no perfect solution.

I think we have to accept certain fundamental realities in Jammu and Kashmir. We have a problem in Jammu and Kashmir — and I don't just mean that we have a problem with India and Pakistan. We have a problem within Jammu and Kashmir. We have a problem of alienation in Jammu and Kashmir, particularly in the Kashmir Valley, amongst Muslim youths around my age-group. I am thirty-three. Add a few years, take away a few years. But that's pretty much the age-group that you are looking at. I appreciate the fact that Mufti Sayeed Sahib mentioned that the leadership on both the sides of the spectrum is young — there can be no denying that. Still we have been unable to make the sort of inroads amongst my age-group to wean it away from the pro-Azadi, or the pro-Pakistan, or the pro-secessionist sentiment, and into what we would traditionally call the nationalist mainstream sentiment. So, you can't wish away internal discontent that exists among the people, and with all due respect, one or two good elections are not the solution. Nor is the solution to talk about a dialogue process, and then sabotage the dialogue process.

When I say this, I refer to the expected dialogue between the Government of India and the Hurriyat Conference. This is a dialogue that, contrary to popular expectations or perceptions, has not been sabotaged by the National Conference. All these years we have wanted a dialogue in Jammu and Kashmir. We have, in fact, strived for a dialogue. The only dialogue between militant groups and a government was during the tenure of our government in Jammu and Kashmir, when Hizb-ul-Mujaheddin announced a ceasefire, and came forward to the dialogue table. But due to reasons that we all know, there was a spurt in violence in two days, the ceasefire was short-lived, and that was the end of it. We are at the threshold of a dialogue process between the separatists — or those perceived to be separatist — and the Government of India.

Now, the only problem with a dialogue like this is that, already we have made it exclusive rather than inclusive. Already, we have made it appear that we are willing to do business with only a particular group of separatists in Jammu and Kashmir, and particularly in Kashmir. And we have managed to split the Hurriyat Conference in two groups — moderates and hardliners. Government of India in its wisdom, has extended the invitation of dialogue to the moderates, but has excluded hardliners from this dialogue process.

The problem I have with this is that we have already made the process that much more difficult than we needed to, because there is a great degree of scepticism about the whole process. The chances of arriving at some sort of understanding with the Hurriyat Conference represented by moderate leaders is extremely slim, but the possibility exists. But tomorrow, when a solution or agreement is arrived at, the first thing you are going to find is that the hardline separatist elements that were excluded from the dialogue are going to be the first ones to criticise it, undermine it, and make sure it doesn't work. And not because they have chosen to stay out of the dialogue process, but because they have been kept out of the dialogue process.

Therefore, if we need to look for a road ahead, I think we need to be very clear on certain points. We can no longer let it appear in the state of Jammu and Kashmir that we are more comfortable doing business with one person, and less comfortable doing business with another — we should not take the onus on ourselves.

As a minister in the Government of India I always felt that one of our biggest failures was that we let, not just the international community, we let our own country believe that the onus was on us to deliver that promised plebiscite in the state of Jammu and Kashmir. I can't tell you how many times I have travelled around this country, and when I have agreed that maybe we can share 50 per cent of the responsibility for not holding a plebiscite in Jammu and Kashmir. But not 100 per cent! And then, when we state the facts about what happened in the United Nations and afterwards, people in our country are amazed. You can imagine the reaction abroad. We have allowed people to believe that it is because of our stubbornness, or our arrogance, that the people in Jammu and Kashmir did not get the plebiscite that was promised to them.

Similarly, with the dialogue process now, we have let it be perceived or understood that, the onus is on us, because we did not invite these individuals to the dialogue. They will avoid talking to us. We should put the onus on them, by indicating, this invitation is for everybody. Let the hardliners not have a reason to not come to the dialogue table. Let us be able to take the upper hand and say, 'We did our best. We went not one step, but ten steps forward. But it was not acceptable, and therefore we have no choice but to confine ourselves to the group that is willing to talk to us.'

There is a yearning for peace in Jammu and Kashmir. How could there not be?

It is difficult to imagine what normal life for people in Jammu and Kashmir is. I'm not going into whether there has been any change on the ground this year, or year and a half. I think that it is for the Chief Minister and myself to slug away at.

Let us assume for a moment that there has been some change on the ground. Has it been enough? No, quite honestly! Do we recognise some of the other fundamental problems in Jammu and Kashmir? I honestly don't believe we do. One realisation that is gradually dawning on me, and which the Chief Minister made a reference to in its historic context, is the concept of *Kashmiriyat*.

It is something that we talk about but seldom understand. If you ask me to talk for fifteen minutes on *Kashmiriyat,* I perhaps would not be able to. It is more of something I feel than something I'm able to express. For, a large part of our *Kashmiriyat* is tolerance for other ideas, ideologies, and religions. And, if you look at the history of Jammu and Kashmir from 1947 onwards, at least till 1990, you will have found that very seldom would you be able to cite an instance here of the sort of communal violence that has plagued other parts of this country.

But over the years, I have gradually begun to be more worried about the fact that the *Kashmiriyat* face of Jammu and

Kashmir is gradually dwindling. The traditional Islamic character of Kashmir is very different from the Islamic character of other countries. The Islam of Kashmir is a Sufiyana Islam. We respect shrines, and we respect saints, which some schools of thought in Islam are against.

Over time, with the availability of money and flow of resources, schools — or what we traditionally call *madrasas* — and a new type of mosque are beginning to emerge in Jammu and Kashmir and are taking root. If not checked, this will — you can mark my words — change the very face of Islam in Jammu and Kashmir. And *not* for the better.

Evidence of this is available in the way the face of militancy in Jammu and Kashmir has changed. Where earlier the youth were attracted with a slogan of *azadi*, or freedom, or a slogan of accretion of Jammu and Kashmir with Pakistan, today much larger numbers of youngsters are going across motivated by the idea of perfecting Islam. They are going across because somebody has convinced them that Islam in Jammu and Kashmir is in danger and it is only if they go across, pick up the gun, come back and save Islam, will they be doing their religion a service.

The problem is that, no matter how many initiatives we take internally, no matter how much of an agreement we arrive at with the Hurriyat Conference, or externally with India and Pakistan, a core feeling takes root in Jammu and Kashmir that, it is not a fight for *azadi* any longer, it is not a fight for Pakistan, but a fight to save Islam. Then no agreement between India and Pakistan, and no agreement between Delhi and Srinagar and Jammu will be able to stop terrorism in Jammu and Kashmir. Because, you will not be able to turn off that tap. I hope somewhere it rings a bell, somewhere it sets off an alarm, and people actually look at the way in which the situation on the ground is changing.

The problem in Kashmir cannot be boxed into one category.It is impossible to suggest that Kashmir is only an internal problem between India and Pakistan. It would also be completely incorrect to suggest Kashmir is only an internal problem and that, if you address the internal alienation then the problem will automatically disappear.The fact is the two go hand in hand.

How much weight you can give to each is something that individuals can disagree upon. But we have seen historically that, when we seek to address one side of the problem and not the other, when we seek to make progress externally while not addressing the internal compulsions, while we seek to bring about external agreements — the Tashkent Agreement, the Simla Agreement, the Lahore Declaration, and perhaps, even if the Agra Declaration had succeeded — but ignore the internal dimension of the problem, we are doomed to failure.

Equally, when we have agreements internally, with the people of Jammu and Kashmir — such as the agreement between Sheikh Abdullah and Pandit Nehru, and the agreement between Sheikh Abdullah and Indira Gandhi — but don't view the problem with its external perspective, we are doomed to failure.

This is perhaps the best opportunity for addressing both the internal and external dimensions simultaneously. Yes, there are certain flaws with the process — and as I mentioned, we need to make sure that this process within Jammu and Kashmir looks inclusive rather than exclusive. I hope the Government of India will make a note of this.

The fact is that, you cannot question a peace dividend for the people of Jammu and Kashmir. What we need to do is to try and reinforce this belief in our neighbour. We need to let Pakistan understand that there *is* a peace dividend for Pakistan as well. Otherwise, what is happening for Pakistan is a very low cost option. It is the easiest way to tie us up in strings and keep us busy. It costs them very little and it seems to reap them rich dividends. I think that premise is one we need to understand. Taking a position — and I took this position for three years — that we will not talk till the last gun is silenced, is not a realistic position, for the simple reason that what does Pakistan have to negotiate with, that would be of interest to India?

I am not a great student of history. I haven't read that many books on Jammu and Kashmir and therefore, you could perhaps find fault with my theoretical knowledge, but on the practical side, if you ask me, we really did not do very much to implement what we agreed upon in Simla. Because there was no onus on us. There was not really much we needed from them (Pakistan). They got their prisoners of war back and there was nothing else to bring to the table. Therefore, we must understand that, what we mainly want from Pakistan today is an end to violence in Jammu and Kashmir. If Pakistan ends violence in Jammu and Kashmir before they come to the dialogue table, we will be less inclined to talk to them.

And therefore, we need to look at a more graded approach. Yes, we understand the last gun cannot be silenced *before* dialogue takes place. That's all right. We accept we will approach this dialogue in a graded manner, in a manner wherein as violence comes down, there will be simultaneously an increase in the level of dialogue and also the depth of that dialogue.

Let us trade in good neighbourly relations. Maintain a bus service between what we call Jammu and Kashmir, and they call Occupied Kashmir, and vice versa. These are all symbolic stepping-stones in the right direction. But we need to be certain of consistency in these measures as well.

The problem is that, through our slogans and statements, we tend to confuse people. When my grandfather (Sheikh Mohammad Abdullah) called for the resumption of a bus service between Srinagar and Muzaffarabad, he was branded Pakistani, he was branded anti-national. It was perceived as if he was trying to convince people of Jammu and Kashmir that they are more a part of Pakistan, and less a part of India. Today, the same people who propose a bus service between Muzaffarabad and Srinagar are perceived to be great nationalist leaders. It's very confusing for people like us. What position am I supposed to take tomorrow?

We need a little consistency in our approach. We also need to be a little less knee-jerk in our reactions.

There are going to be serious hurdles ahead internally within Jammu and Kashmir, and also between the two countries. There are large constituencies that don't want peace in Jammu and Kashmir. Let us not for a moment believe that we are only talking about the militant element in Jammu and Kashmir — it will do everything to sabotage the peace process. But you will be amazed how much of a vested interest has developed within the system in Jammu and Kashmir that does not want peace there. You would be amazed, and I shudder to think, when I recall conversations I've had with responsible people in government, wherein they have told me that if you ever believe that we will allow peace to return to Jammu and Kashmir you're fooling yourself. And I ask them why, and they tell me: 'You'll shut off our eating and drinking.'

The amount of unaccounted money that flows into Jammu and Kashmir in the name of anti-militancy operations is unbelievable. I would probably be disclosing a national secret if I explained to you just how much money the chief minister has at his disposal that, he doesn't have to account for — and that's at his level. It trickles right down the system to the police officer in-charge of a police post. The officer has at his disposal a monthly amount of money he's supposed to pay to renegades, to gather information. Do you think he wants peace in Jammu and Kashmir? Do you think he wants a situation where that money will be turned off? He perhaps thinks this is an excellent thing, to have X amount of money to pay out, whereby he will project a payment of X amount, and actually he would only pay 50 per cent of that. Fifty per cent goes into his pocket. Who is going to budget that? Even today in Punjab, the police make claims for security-related expenditure. When was the last time any of you heard about a militant attack in Punjab?

So, we are up against a very tough opposition. Let us not for a moment assume that the road ahead is easy — externally and internally we are up against all sorts of factors. But I think we need the strength of character and the depth of leadership that, perhaps till now has been missing. I think we need a commonality of interests on both sides of the border.

Both India and Pakistan have to realise that there is no other solution in their best interests than the resolution of the Jammu and Kashmir issue, and peace between our two countries. I know how we talk about good relations between India and Sri Lanka, or good relations between India and Nepal, or Bangladesh, but our good relations with these countries are held hostage more times than we would like to believe, due to bad relations between India and Pakistan. How many times have we called off SAARC summits because India and Pakistan have been unable to sit at the same table? And I daresay, how many times in the future are these things going to happen?

When I said we need to be less knee-jerk, I meant we need to institutionalise the process. We can't afford to turn on the tap of dialogue, and then when a militant attack takes place, turn the tap off again. We have to accept that there is going to be a rise in the level of militancy if this dialogue process is going to reach its culmination. Because, you have maybe 4,000 (militants) on the ground in Jammu and Kashmir today, who, if tomorrow peace were established between India and Pakistan, would be orphaned. Neither India nor Pakistan would be willing to own them. Do you think they have any stake in a peace between India and Pakistan? No! And therefore, they will do their utmost to ensure that peace will not emerge. And therefore, we have to be willing to accept that there will be a certain amount of increase in violence as this peace process goes on.

We need to have the political will to be able to withstand that. We have to be able to tell the people, "Look, I know at this point you want me to stop the dialogue process. You want me to start beating the war drums with Pakistan again, but I'm not going to!" We've tried the military options for a solution between India and Pakistan. We've tried the violent option of crushing the militants in Jammu and Kashmir as well. Neither has reaped us very rich dividends.

I will end with this simple belief that people in Jammu and Kashmir are yearning for peace. The makings of a process, both internally and externally are present. Both are extremely fragile. Both are literally a hair's breadth away from breaking again and therefore, we need to be careful about how we approach the situation, what we say and what we do.

In ensuring peace in Jammu and Kashmir there can be no divisions or divides between Mufti Sayeed Sahib and myself, and our parties, no matter how divided we are on day-to-day issues of water, electricity and the rest of it!

There is a peace dividend to be gained by all of us, and I hope we have the strength of character to actually see this process through, and deliver the results.

Q & A: Kashmir

Q: Mr Chief Minister, you talked about problems and also about a lot of things that were not possible in Kashmir, but you failed somehow to say what was possible. You said the Line of Control could not be the border, and there may not be ready answers, but could you please propose a solution?

Mufti Mohammad Sayeed: The position of both countries, our country and Pakistan is very clear. Our position is Kashmir is the core of Indian nationhood. Pakistan's claim is that Kashmir is the life-vein of Pakistan. So both stands can't be reconciled immediately. You can find some solution through an evolutionary process, by removing the walls of hatred between the people of two countries. There is no formula, no readymade solution to a problem that could not be solved these past fifty-three years, a problem that even Pandit Jawaharlal Nehru could not solve. But there should be a movement forward. We should not be pessimistic. Where there is a will, there is a way.

Q: The question is for both of you. There is tremendous development taking place in India, or the rest of India if I were to say this from Kashmir's perspective. In Kashmir, development cannot proceed at that pace because of the conflict. What do you see as the problem in achieving a similar economic development in Kashmir, which has, due to its circumstances, lost maybe 10 years?

Omar Abdullah: It's a chicken and egg story, isn't it? What comes first, development or peace? Gone are the days when the Government of India could invest large sums of money in public sector undertakings, and generate employment. Largely this is now the job of the private sector. You can't expect the private sector to put money in a situation where they're not sure that their returns of investment are going to be safe. And therefore that is the problem that we're grappling with.

I'll give you a small example. I took three years working in the Government of India to get a package of incentives approved for Jammu and Kashmir for investment. And it was three years of hard work wherein we finally succeeded. Six months down the line, when we started getting investment opportunities and proposals, the Government of India, for some unknown reason, announced the same package of incentives for Himachal Pradesh, Uttaranchal, and a couple of other states. Everybody who was looking at Jammu and Kashmir moved to Himachal and Uttaranchal for a simple reason. Why would you invest in Jammu and Kashmir when you could invest in Uttaranchal, which I think is 100 kms from Noida? These are the sort of problems we are grappling with.

We need to be realistic about what we want to achieve. There was no need to make that package available to Himachal and Uttaranchal six months after Kashmir. I don't want to deny them that package—wait two years, three years. You waited five years in the case of the North-eastern states. Why not do the same favour for Jammu and Kashmir?

We need to understand that if economic activity has to be developed , people are not going to come forward on their own. They need to be encouraged, and for that, government needs to get its act together.

India's **Roadmap** FOR PEACE

Sonia Gandhi

‘The warp and weft of our social fabric, our collective DNA, as it were, is composed of many religions languages, ethnic groups and cultures living with each other. They derive support and sustenance from each other. We have to rediscover the well-springs of reconciliation both within our societies, and across our political borders.’

Sonia Gandhi

President, Congress Party & Leader of the Opposition, Parliament of India

The theme of this get-together has perennial relevance. But in the current circumstances, the timing could not have been more apt.

The winds of peace and goodwill are once again blowing in our region. Friendship is in the air. Yet another new beginning appears to be on the horizon.

It is easy to be cynical. It is natural to be cautious.

But we must hope that this phase is longer lasting and will set the stage for a new future for South Asia, a future which over a billion and a quarter people are entitled to.

I have been asked to speak on the Indian roadmap. Before I do so, let me briefly go over some of the more crucial challenges that confront us collectively in this region.

Our societies are rich tapestries, tapestries that reflect a long tradition of syncretism. The warp and weft of our social fabric, our collective DNA, as it were, is composed of many religions, languages, ethnic groups, and cultures living with each other. They derive support and sustenance from each other. They contribute to and enrich each other.

The recent past may have kept us apart but we have a common future. We have to rediscover the well-springs of reconciliation both within our societies and across our political borders.

The fundamental task we face is to create an all-inclusive social architecture in which there is no place for bigotry, for intolerance, for obscurantism of any kind. Once when asked by Andre Malraux what his greatest challenge was, Jawaharlal

 Nehru replied, "To build a just society by just means and to establish a secular state in a religious society." That challenge is very much before us today.

And how will this architecture come about?

- It will come about through representative, liberal democracy.
- It will result from economic development that is both efficient and equitable.
- It will be the outcome of respecting social diversity.
- And it will emerge from a sustained dialogue across different divides.

Our nation-states have been far too centralised. That had a logic at a particular point of time over half a century ago. Today, what we need is a multi-tiered democracy, an empowered and decentralised democracy. There is no other system which is both representative and durable, both accountable and transparent.

Our economies have performed well in recent times. But not well enough to deal with the huge backlog of poverty, malnutrition, disease and unemployment. There is no alternative to faster economic growth. There is no alternative to an effective role for the state in this transformation.

Our social systems have been subject to many fissures. The feeling of alienation has grown. Violence has become endemic in many parts. Within the parameters of political unity and territorial integrity, what is needed is a sensitive approach to heal wounds. The profound consequences of migration, both within and across our countries, have to be dealt with humanely.

Our polities are filled with discord and the areas of agreement have shrunk. What is now needed is a determined search for common ground, a serious pursuit of a consensus that allows us to move ahead, even while having differences.

Our societies must have institutions for dialogue, a dialogue that comes to terms with our past, a dialogue that provides a framework for living in the present and realising the future.

What about India's own contribution? What would be the configuration of our ICBMs—Indian Confidence Building Measures, I hasten to add?

India has an important role to play. Further, it must play a consistent role, a role that is always sensitive to the needs and concerns of its neighbours.

At the same time, I believe we have every right to expect that our neighbours will not allow themselves to become sanctuaries for those who unleash their deadly tools of terror against innocent men, women and children in our country. Indeed, as neighbours all of us must ensure that our territories are not havens for those who seek legitimacy through violence.

The demographic and physical size of India invites a degree of apprehension. But that need not be so if India has a positive agenda that emphasises mutually beneficial outcomes.

We have consistently been in favour of engaging constructively with Pakistan on all issues under the Simla Agreement and subsequent accords. That we can work together for the common good in spite of all vicissitudes is revealed by the durability of the 1960 Indus Waters Treaty.

India, China and Pakistan should evolve a credible and transparent mechanism to manage the consequences of a nuclear South Asia.

The huge eastern Himalayan river basin needs to be developed quickly by India, Nepal, Bangladesh and Bhutan.

A South Asian Free Trade Area ought to be in place by 2005, and an economic community by the middle of the next decade.

India and Bangladesh should establish a bilateral framework for closer cooperation as well as a regional one that embraces Myanmar, Thailand and provinces of China.

We share the hopes and desires of Sri Lanka that its ethnic strife comes to an end, and an agreed power-sharing and devolution arrangement is put in place soon.

The unique ecology of the Maldives has to be preserved and protected.

India can provide an impetus to improving and expanding road, rail and air connectivity in the entire region, and in developing cross-country tourism circuits.

India can take the initiative in sharing its considerable expertise in areas like information technology and biotechnology to improve governance, and transform agriculture on which our shared prosperity rests.

India must continue to pursue closer political and economic ties with China as it has done since 1988. While this has a logic of its own, a deeper Sino-Indian relationship has a positive impact on our immediate neighbourhood.

Most of all, India has to remain an outstanding example of an open liberal, pluralistic democracy, committed to secular values, committed to combating religious fundamentalism of all kinds, committed to preserving and protecting its composite heritage. We must fight those forces that seek to use regional tension to polarise our own society.

When I say India should play an important role, it is not just a role for the Government of India or even for some of our State governments. Institutions of civil society—like NGOs, universities, think tanks, hospitals, media, professional associations, industrialists, sports bodies—also have a leadership role to play. Just think of the tremendous outpouring of sympathy that accompanied Noor Fatima's journey from Lahore to Bangalore in search of a new life.

Over time, why can't we for instance, conceive of a South Asian Parliament as a permanent deliberative body on issues of regional concern and importance? Such a body could expand the perspective on South Asia among all our countries. Incidentally, I should mention here this was a little-noticed idea contained in our election manifesto for the 1999 Lok Sabha elections.

And what about SAARC?The posturing at SAARC hits the headlines. But not enough credit is given to the initiatives that have been taken. Eleven summits have been held in the past thirteen years and the twelfth is to be held soon in Islamabad. Each of the Summit Declarations is a mission statement in itself. If implemented with a single-minded sense of collective purpose, they can transform our region.

- SAARC regional centres in crucial areas like weather forecasting and health have been established.
- A SAARC food security reserve has been built up.
- SAARC conventions in critical areas like prostitution, child welfare and narcotics control have been adopted.

- SAARC networks have been created in diverse fields like economic research, media, law, accountancy, management, town planning and in trade and business.

Independent commissions on poverty alleviation have been set up. Groups of Wise Men (alas, no wise women, as yet!) have been mobilised.

But I have to admit that SAARC is not given the same importance by all of us as we accord to other bilateral, regional and international bodies. Not all of this is of India's making, but the need for a whole new mindset on SAARC in our country cannot be denied. As a beginning why should India not take a bold step to substantially increase the core capital base of the South Asia Development Fund that now stands at a paltry US$6 million?

Looking beyond SAARC, South Asia's unique culture and geography give it a special trans-regional positioning as well. It is linked to West Asia in many ways. It has been associated intimately with central Asia. It is now building new partnerships in East Asia. From every point of view—investment, trade, energy, labour markets, these linkages must be deepened. Collaboration with ASEAN, the Shanghai Cooperation Organisation and the Gulf Cooperation Council must be essential on security-related issues. The time may also have come to think in terms of a South Asian Security Forum.

May I say a few words on the gifted and talented sub-continental diaspora that has come into prominence in recent years in many countries? Their achievements are a source of pride for all of us.This diaspora can be a great force for good, for building bridges. But there is a dark side to this as well—we all know how dangerous long-distance, offshore nationalism can be. We have experience of both the positive and the negative impact of overseas communities on domestic politics and social relations.

Our attempt must be to proliferate the positive and take concentrated steps to ensure that we are not diverted by the negative. The real hope lies in the new generation of the diaspora that is in a better position to free itself from the shackles of the past and become the harbinger of a new South Asia.

Is there a role for the international community to help us reap the peace dividend? Most decidedly yes, even though the primary responsibility remains ours.

We need a system of globalisation that is sensitive to the great dependence of our countries on agriculture. This system has to be responsive to the huge demands we face to create productive jobs year after year. It must also mitigate the risks inherent in the process of international integration.

We need international financing of critical cross-country infrastructure projects.

While trade will be an engine of growth, there will still be need for development assistance in vital areas like health and the environment.

Most of all, we need the world community to appreciate the extraordinary complexity and depth of the challenges we confront.

Q & A: Sonia Gandhi

Q: To what extent do the initiatives being deployed by our prime minister—he also spoke very forcefully of the dividends of peace, peace initiatives—have bipartisan support? And as Leader of the Opposition, or your party, how often and how effectively are you consulted in the formulation of our national foreign policy?

Sonia Gandhi: Well as far as the initiatives taken by the government are concerned, specifically by the prime minister, such as initiating a dialogue with Pakistan, we have been supportive. I would say very supportive from the very beginning. In fact, I can say that even when the government was not keen on initiating a dialogue at a certain point with Pakistan, our party always maintained that it was important to have a formal or informal opening of discussion. We raised this initiative again and again at our political forums, in parliament, and privately. So, there is no doubt here about our support to the government.

As far as the second question goes, I would say yes and no. We are consulted at times, but not always.

Q: Are you consulted more often or not consulted more often?

Sonia Gandhi: I would say that perhaps more often we are not consulted. Or, let us say we are consulted when decisions have already been taken. So there isn't much we can say or much part we can play in that. Yes, we are more informed but it is not always so. Let's not be too harsh.

Q: When your party decided about a year and a half or so ago that Mufti Mohammad Sayeed will form the government in Jammu and Kashmir and he will be the Chief Minister, I think the whole country applauded your statesman-like decision. Could you share with us at least some of your experiences and thoughts on this kind of a coalition, and your vision?

Sonia Gandhi: Yes, I am happy with the role we played in giving the possibility to the PDP (Peoples' Democratic Party) to form a government. I took that decision because I believe it was in the larger interest of Jammu and Kashmir and of the country. I must add, it wasn't a very easy decision to come to but I have no regrets. As you probably know, we have a common minimum programme, which has been worked out mutually.

I am fairly satisfied with the progress of the government but we are faced with tremendous challenges. There are huge expectations. There are challenges of unemployment, of lack of social and physical structure and many other challenges. But I, on the whole, am satisfied even though we have worked much harder in order to deliver what we promised to the people of Jammu and Kashmir during the elections.

As far as the 'healing touch' policy goes, yes, the Chief Minister of Jammu and Kashmir has initiated it and I do believe that it is important to have dialogue with all sections of society, and to hear from them what they feel, what they want. I believe this is important particularly if we want to lessen a certain feeling of alienation, which does exist in the (Kashmir) Valley in particular.

Q: Your party has been defeated in three very important states. And, you have not made a secret of the fact that you regard the BJP as a fundamentalist party with very divisive politics. What are the implications, both for India and for the region, with this defeat of the Congress? Also, the implications for Congress after these defeats?

Sonia Gandhi: During the last elections, the BJP lost its faith. Well, we lost it this time. I have expressed my disappointment; I think all of you, if you were in my place, would feel pretty much the same. To a large extent, particularly in two states, heavy anti-incumbency factor played a big role in our losing the elections. I think there was also weakness in our campaign. To a certain extent, perhaps, we also went wrong in the distribution of tickets. This has served as a big lesson, and we will do our best to rectify this. I have already held a meeting of the Congress Working Committee to discuss and to hear from my colleagues who were involved in the election, what they felt went wrong. At the same time, there is absolutely no doubt we have to rectify these weaknesses, especially because as you say, we have to prepare ourselves for the big battle ahead, probably next year, against fundamentalism ... the party, the government, which is in place.

Q: Which State was the biggest surprise?

Sonia Gandhi: For me the biggest surprise was Rajasthan.

Q: Why Rajasthan? Why not Chattisgarh? Why not Madhya Pradesh?

Sonia Gandhi: Well, Madhya Pradesh because of the double anti-incumbency. We were there for two terms, ten long years. If you look at it closely, till three years ago, when Chattisgarh was created, we were in Madhya Pradesh. So, there is a certain amount of double anti-incumbency there. But in Rajasthan, I felt, the government had done a great deal of good work. So, that was a surprise to me though at the end, I knew it was going to be a tough or close fight. But I did think that we would win.

Q: Do you think they (the BJP) fought a much better campaign in Rajasthan than you did?

Sonia Gandhi: Surely. The fact is they won. Particularly in the last week, they were much more aggressive and proactive and we could not match that. I would also like to add that we may have lost some of these places but there has been a great deal of work in all the States in terms of development and social infrastructure, though much less in physical infrastructure, like electricity infrastructure—and that is why we lost. This fact has been recognised; I am aware of the good work that has been done, but obviously it was not enough.

Q: Why do you think you won in Delhi?

Sonia Gandhi: Delhi was won because of performance and good governance. But of course, Delhi is a much easier State to win. And, of course, Sheila Dikshit has definitely done a great job. She had done a great deal of good work in the state.

Securing South Asia

Lakshman Kadirgamar
Asfandyar Wali Khan
Richard Haass

'Today, if any of us were to see our destiny as lying along the path of engagement with others outside the region as well as with our neighbours within South Asia, it cannot reasonably be argued that thereby South Asian unity would be denied or diminished.'

Lakshman Kadirgamar

Former Minister of Foreign Affairs, Sri Lanka;
Adviser on Foreign Affairs to the
President of Sri Lanka

Today, when we speak of the security of a state we no longer mean its physical security alone. When we speak of strategy we no longer mean military or defence strategy alone. The concepts of security and strategy have acquired a much wider connotation. They involve all matters relating to the maintenance of the stability and the enhancement of the prosperity of a country and of the region in which that country is situated. The ongoing process of globalisation has inculcated an awareness of interdependence among countries, certainly in regional terms, if not yet fully in global terms.

Thus, political instability in a country threatens not only its own security but the security of its neighbours. So also with financial and economic instability; whereas bilateral or multilateral trading and fiscal arrangements, defence pacts and other forms of conventional military collaboration, would tend to promote national and regional security. When we address the subject of 'securing South Asia' we must, therefore, necessarily contemplate not the security of individual states in isolation, in a parochial sense, but the security of South Asia as a whole, in a collective sense.

I wish to place a possible conceptual framework within which the question of securing South Asia could be considered.

First, the political will to forge a cohesive and concerted association amongst ourselves is the very essence of regional security and cooperation. Second, the measure of regional security and of regional cooperation then becomes the degree to which we are able to agree about the intrinsic character of our region, where we each stand in relation to the others, what the impact is upon us, severally and collectively, of the prevailing external order, and how best we should respond thereto. And third, in my view the only way to such agreement, if indeed it can ever be achieved, is to talk freely and frankly to each other, in order to minimise, hopefully eliminate, misunderstanding and achieve mutual trust and confidence.

Today, across the globe, regional groupings tend to overlap because shared economic and political interests among discontiguous neighbours tend to converge. Thus, today if any of us were to see our destiny as lying along the path of engagement with others outside the region, as well as with our neighbours within South Asia, it cannot reasonably be argued that thereby, South Asian unity would be denied or diminished. Each of us is a member of some other grouping to which all of us do not belong. However, if our regional unity is to be preserved and promoted, each regional member-state must address this core issue of political will from the standpoint of its own situation. I mean by that, its geographical location, historical experience, and chosen national aspirations. If the process of addressing that core issue can, nonetheless, be undertaken collectively, then the prospects of reaching agreement, and thereby of forging regional cohesion would stand greatly enhanced.

That is why we in Sri Lanka—and this is conspicuously a shared approach among all our political parties and throughout our citizenry—lay such store by developing a process of free and frank exchanges amongst our neighbours to facilitate the process of addressing that core issue of collective political will. It is to that same end that I direct myself on this occasion, by attempting to provide you with a Sri Lankan perception of the region, and of where we stand within it. Let me first try to identify what I perceive to be certain unchangeable and inescapable regional realities, and then say something about our own regional position. Thereafter, against the backdrop of the conceptual framework that I am laying before you I will draw attention to certain developments that are taking place in Sri Lanka which could threaten the legitimate interests of India and thus affect the security of South Asia collectively.

The first regional reality is India's preponderance over all others in South Asia. It is a preponderance based upon size, resources, development and power, allied to influence. A second reality is India's unique centrality. Also, with each of her neighbours India has special ties—whether of ethnicity, language, culture and kinship, or of common historical experience, or of shared access to and dependence upon vital natural resources—of a character and to a degree of intensity which is not shared by any two others. There is a third reality, which bears directly upon the other two. It is the co-terminality of the national borders of regional member-states with those great natural physical barriers, which encompass South Asia—the Himalayas and the Indian Ocean.

I believe it is fair to say that probably no other region in the world presents such an integral security zone. The force of that point may perhaps be the better appreciated if one were to consider the analogy of a wheel. At its hub lies regionally preponderant India. Radiating as spokes are India's regional neighbours, with each of whom India shares land or maritime boundaries, but no two others are thus joined without at the same time touching India also. Binding those spokes to that hub are the physical barriers which I mentioned. Recognition of this characteristic, of the security of the region being an integer, a thing complete in itself, was of course central to the administration of the British Raj. Given her preponderance and centrality within the region it would not be surprising, indeed it would be wholly logical, if India viewed her security along similar lines. That is to say, in my view India may justifiably regard any alien presence or influence within those natural security borders, which was not there with her own acquiescence, as a potential threat to her national security.

I said earlier that each regional member-state was likely to view both the region and its place in it from the particular standpoint of its own national situation. Having briefly indicated how the region appears to a Sri Lankan, let me say something of where Sri Lanka stands, within the region. We are a small island exposed to a vast ocean on all sides, upon and beneath which man and his machines, benign or evil, may undertake ventures beyond our limited ken. At the northern tip of our island, we share a maritime boundary with our only visible neighbour, so to speak, across a waterway no wider than a mere short dash by fiberglass boat with outboard motors. That neighbour also happens to be one of the world's largest, most populous and potentially powerful nations. The proximity of India, the 'India factor', if one may so describe it, is a cardinal factor in our lives as a nation. There is of course much more to that India factor than the proximity of neighbourliness. To begin with, there is no other neighbour equally powerful and proximal to countervail India. Then, there is India's huge advantage in disparity of resources, levels of development, power and influence globally. We have with her the widest interaction between peoples and governments, and it thus lies with her to help or hinder us to the greatest extent.

In this context there are three elements of the 'India factor' which vitally affect governance in Sri Lanka. First, when our domestic political and military problems descend into crisis, we would be well advised, as indeed major world powers have advised us publicly, that India being indisputably the pre-eminent regional power, with a special responsibility for regional stability, to avail ourselves of that factor: namely, of India's help in resolving any of our internal crises. The second element is the Tamil connection between ourselves and Indian Tamils, principally in the state of Tamil Nadu, but also elsewhere in India. The third element is what I may call the 'backyard concept', that is to say that Sri Lanka is India's exposed southern flank.

With regard to the second element, the large Tamil population in South India gives India a special concern with the Sri Lanka Tamil question. Let me emphasise my view, however, that to concede such a special concern is by no means to acquiesce in unwarranted Indian interference in our affairs, as such. It must, nonetheless, be recognised that, if the situation of Sri Lankan Tamils becomes seriously disadvantaged, no Indian government of the day can shut its eyes to that situation and those consequences, because the spillover effect of those consequences on Tamil Nadu would inevitably and compulsively engage the attention of the government of that state and the central government of the day. Hence, it is an obvious conclusion that ideally the Tamil question within our polity should be so managed as to preclude the need for Indian concern, far less involvement. However, it would be wholly unrealistic for anyone to claim that under no circumstances could India have a legitimate concern with the management of certain aspects of our internal affairs.

The third element stems from our own geographical location vis-à-vis India. As I said, Sri Lanka is India's exposed southern flank. It thereby becomes a matter of vital concern for India as to who comes and goes, and what happens, in Sri Lanka. The point of interconnection is this. Should for instance, a Sri Lankan government of the day, facing an internal crisis concerning the Tamils there, be seen by India to engage the involvement, especially the military involvement of any other regional member, far worse an outside power altogether in its resolution, then it would be only fair to surmise that the Indian government of that day will be hard put, whatever moral underpinning is cited to the contrary, to keep its gaze firmly averted in an attitude of studied nonchalance.

No Sri Lankan would presume to suggest that this subjective view should be regarded as an objective yardstick of measurement for use by any other regional partner. It is advanced here as no more than an aid to discussion amongst us, of the region, and in the region. The bottom line of regional security and of cooperation will always remain that measure of agreement which we are able to achieve in synthesising our respective national perceptions about the region's relationship to the wider world beyond. But to construct a meaningful regionalism in South Asia, we have no other option but to test those national perceptions against each other's in free, frank and accommodating discussion, which is at all times informed by an evident desire to find common ground.

If we are able to forge an effective regionalism, built upon and around the strengths of our region, and present to the demanding world beyond a cohesive and concerted collectivity, I believe the rewards would be significant, for each and all of us. If we fail in that endeavour, undoubtedly some amongst us would be able to survive and even to prosper. Others, though, will stand deeply disadvantaged. For the small and weak amongst us, there can be no question but that regionalism is our future. The question that the bigger and stronger amongst us must surely address is whether or not their own future would also stand enhanced or retarded by joining with the others in that regional exercise. I believe strongly that it would.

In 1996, India's minister of external affairs, Mr I.K. Gujral, delivered a speech, 'Foreign Policy Objectives of India's United Front Government', at the Royal Institute of International Affairs in London. It was a speech of majestic sweep, elegant and refined and, above all, of almost startling candour.

In that London speech, in a passage of enormous significance for the whole region, Mr Gujral made a commitment of political will on the part of India to mitigate the impact of the asymmetries I referred to earlier.

"The United Front government's neighbourhood policy now stands on five basic principles: First, with the neighbours like Nepal, Bangladesh, Bhutan, Maldives and Sri Lanka, India does not ask for reciprocity but gives all that it can in good faith and trust. Secondly, no South Asian country will allow its territory to be used against the interest of another country of the region. Thirdly, none will interfere in the internal affairs of another. Fourthly, all South Asians must respect each other's territorial integrity and sovereignty. And finally, they will settle all their disputes through peaceful, bilateral negotiations. These five principles, scrupulously observed, will, I am sure, recast South Asia's regional relationships, including the tormented relationship between India and Pakistan, in a friendly, cooperative mould."

I was heartened to read, early this year, that Mr Yashwant Sinha, India's current minister of external affairs, had endorsed these principles, thus giving them extended bipartisan validity. In my opinion, each of those five propositions is intrinsically sound. Each is wise. Each is capable of implementation. Taken collectively, they constitute a practical and principled foundation for regional cooperation and security. In my Krishna Menon Memorial Centenary lecture delivered in December 1996, when I was the minister of foreign affairs of Sri Lanka, I endorsed those propositions without reservation, and seven years later I do so again. I express the hope, the fervent hope of all of us in the other five countries of the region, that India and Pakistan will see in these principles the way forward for them on the path of friendship and peace.

How often, when I was chairman of the SAARC Council of Ministries for three years—the longest period that chair has been occupied by one country—did I feel myself in the grip of helpless frustration, striving to keep SAARC afloat, let alone keep it moving when the rest of us were held hostage to yet another breakdown in India-Pakistan relations. Sri Lanka remains institutionally loyal to the Simla Declaration—the dispute between India and Pakistan is an internal matter to be resolved by them and between them. But by the same token, my silent plea used to be: please resolve the matter, or at least reach a sensible accommodation so that we might all move forward together in a world of limitless opportunities to a future of incredible promise for all of us in South Asia.

I am, and have always been, an ardent, indeed an unrepentant, devotee of South Asian cooperation and unity. I believe that cooperation instead of conflict, cooperation that dispels mistrust, is not only desirable because without it our future is bleak and fruitless, but if we move towards cooperation and unity we will surely unleash, and then collectively harness, for the good of the entire region the undeniably vast potential of our richly endowed subcontinent. I have spoken on this theme often, but I never tire of returning to it because I am convinced that the diverse peoples of our sub-continent hunger for the friendship of their cousins and an end to estrangement. If, for holding this view, I am dubbed a romantic I accept that appellation as a badge of honour.

I turn now to the specific situation of Sri Lanka in respect firstly, of ground realities and secondly, evolving political developments. I will draw your attention to six points with regard to the military situation.

1. A ceasefire was signed in February 2002. There have been no armed clashes since that date, but the LTTE has committed numerous violations both in spirit and letter of the ceasefire, by continuing to smuggle in arms by sea (two arms ships were sunk, but many have got through), committing extortion in the name of taxation, conscripting underage children (well documented by international agencies), assassinating political opponents, harassing Muslims in the East, considerably expanding the strength of its armed cadres, establishing a separate judicial system, banks, police stations, etc.
2. The LTTE has had for many years, and continues to expand, a so-called navy, which consists of a large number of small boats of various kinds driven by outboard motors.
3. The security of Trincomalee harbour, one of the world's best and deepest natural harbours, has been severely compromised. A large number of camps and other LTTE military installations have arisen around the southern rim of the harbour since the ceasefire. The strength of LTTE cadres in that area is estimated above 2,000. Mobile field artillery capable of reaching targets 17 kilometres away have been sighted in the area together with large quantities of 105 mm, 85 mm and 82 mm mortars and other types of weapons. The famous naval dockyard built by the British is within range of field artillery. Suicide boats hidden in the mangrove swamps of the inner rim of the harbour have been spotted. The harassment of Muslims who live on the rim of the harbour has increased in order to drive them away. The large collection of oil tanks built by the British, which have now been leased to the Indian Oil Corporation, are situated on the rim of the harbour.
4. A fact finding mission from the US Pacific Command in Hawai concluded last year that the presence of the LTTE camps and artillery on the rim of the harbour could lead

to the Sri Lankan Navy being "leveled". They recommended that the southern rim should be cleared of LTTE positions as otherwise Trincomalee harbour would become indefensible.

5. In a debate in the Sri Lankan parliament on 8th October 2003, the then Minister of Defence (who was subsequently removed from office) stated, in reply to my speech, that since the ceasefire the LTTE has "nearly doubled" its strength in the area, and he agreed with me that the real threat to the harbour came from its artillery.
6. It will be noted that major international shipping lanes pass the east coast of Sri Lanka and are therefore rendered vulnerable if Trincomalee harbour should fall into the hands of the LTTE.

In assessing the threat to regional security and especially to the security of India, let alone Sri Lanka, posed by the threat to the Trincomalee harbour the following considerations need to be kept in mind:

a) The presence of a third so-called navy in the region, however rudimentary it might be for the moment, poses a threat to Sri Lanka and India that cannot be discounted. A retired Indian admiral speaking at a seminar in Colombo recently drew pointed attention to this naval threat.
b) Since India now has a legal stake in the oil tanks by virtue of their lease to the Indian Oil Corporation, the security of the oil tanks becomes a matter of direct concern to India.
c) In the event of hostilities the China Bay Air Force base on the rim of the Trincomalee harbour is likewise rendered vulnerable and so is the Palaly Air Force base in the northern province. The LTTE's ambition to develop a rudimentary air force is well known.

I move next to the evolving political situation in Sri Lanka.

On 1 November 2003, after twenty years of intermittent warfare, the LTTE for the first time made proposals for the settlement of our problem. They have asked for the establishment of an Internal Self Governing Authority (ISGA). While they agreed at Oslo in December 2002 to explore a federal solution "based upon the principle of internal self-determination in the areas of historical habitation of the Tamil speaking peoples within a united Sri Lanka", their recent proposals go far beyond the parameters of any known federal model.

I wish to highlight a number of points with regard to the LTTE proposals:

1. *The 26-paragraph preamble reveals the LTTE's mindset.* There is reference to the right to self-determination of peoples; to the LTTE's determination to establish an ISGA for the north-east to provide for the urgent needs of the people by formulating laws and policies and effectively and expeditiously executing development while the process for reaching a final settlement is ongoing; to a resolution of 1976 of the Federal Party, adopted twenty-seven years ago, which mandated the elected representatives of the Tamil people to establish an independent sovereign secular state for the Tamil people; to the LTTE exercising effective control and jurisdiction over the majority of the north-east area of Sri Lanka which is factually incorrect; to the need for raising revenue to meet the urgent needs of rehabilitation etc and for carrying out any functions of the government, and to the importance of control over land.

   There are hugely significant statements and omissions in the proposals, which affect the sovereignty of the State of Sri Lanka and violate the Constitution.
2. *Clause 9. Jurisdiction of the ISGA.* The ISGA will have "plenary powers" for the governance of the north-east. Governance, by any definition, includes security and defence. "Plenary" means absolute, unqualified. By seeking "plenary powers" the LTTE wants unqualified and absolute powers of governance over the north-east without any organic link with the Sri Lankan state. The executive power of the people, including defence, which is vested in the President under Article 4 (b) of the Constitution will thus be seriously eroded.
3. *There is no reference to parliament or its role in relation to the ISGA.* As noted earlier, a significant pointer to the

complete marginalisation of parliament is the preambular reference to the ISGA formulating laws.

4. *Clause 10. Separation of Powers.* There is no reference to the Supreme Court or to the present judicial structure of Sri Lanka. On the contrary, Clause 10 says that "separate institutions for the administration of justice shall be established for the north-east, and judicial power shall be vested in such institutions." Therefore, there will not be one Supreme Court for the sovereign State of Sri Lanka. Under Article 3 of the Constitution sovereignty is in the people and is inalienable. Under Article 4 (c) the judicial power of the people shall be exercised by parliament through courts etc created, established or recognised by the Constitution or by law. Thus, Clause 10 of the proposals clearly violates the Constitution.
5. *Clause 11. The ISGA will have total control of financial matters excluding the Government.* But the Government is expected to make contributions to the ISGA budget from the Consolidated Fund although the Government will have no control over the expenditure of such funds.
6. *Clause 12. Powers to borrow, receive aid and trade.* The ISGA will have powers to borrow internally and externally, provide guarantees and indemnities, receive aid directly and engage in and regulate internal and external trade— there is no reference to the government in this cluster of powers.
7. *Clause 13. Accounting and auditing of funds.* The ISGA will appoint a separate Auditor General. This violates Article 153 of the Constitution. Under the Constitution there is only one Auditor General. This is a clear indication that parliament will have no say in the affairs of the ISGA.
8. *Clause 16.* With the demand that all occupied land in the north-east be immediately vacated the government's role in security is considerably eroded. In this event, Palaly Airport, in particular, will be left defenceless and the Trincomalee Harbour will be in grave peril.
9. *Clause 18. Marine and off-shore resources.* The ISGA shall have control over the marine and offshore resources of

adjacent seas and power to regulate access thereto. If control over the marine and offshore resources of the adjacent seas passes to the ISGA, the territorial integrity and sovereignty of the State of Sri Lanka will be very considerably compromised. There will be a grave threat to international shipping lanes that pass the east coast of Sri Lanka, and needless to say to the security interests of India. The power sought by the LTTE to "regulate access" means that the Sri Lankan navy will no longer be able to regulate access to the adjacent seas and will therefore not be able to perform its duty to protect the territorial integrity of the state. It must be remembered that the coastline of the seas adjacent to the north-east go all the way down to Hambantota in the east (the southern tip of Sri Lanka), and to Mannar or below in the west. The north-east coastline comprises almost two-thirds of the coast of Sri Lanka.

10. *Clauses 20 and 22. Water Use and Settlement of Disputes.* The provisions relating to water use and the settlement of disputes between the GOSL and the LTTE, especially the requirement of parity of status, clearly show that the LTTE is preparing the legal ground for a separate state.
11. *Clause 3. Elections.* The provision dealing with elections is also an extremely important indication of the LTTE's possible ultimate objective. It says that if after five years of the envisaged agreement coming into force, no final settlement has been reached and implemented, then an independent election commission appointed by the ISGA shall conduct a free and fair election. This is the clause that conceals the power or right to secede. The LTTE can say after five years – "no agreement has been reached, we will hold an election," and then declare a separate state having explained to the world why, as the preamble indicates, they were driven to take that ultimate step. The fault for not reaching a final settlement, acceptable to the LTTE, would be attributed solely to the government. As long as the LTTE remains heavily armed, no free and fair election can possibly be held.

12. *The removal of the governor from the north-east power structure violates the 13th amendment to the Constitution.*
13. *The composition of the ISGA.* The salient features are: There will be members appointed by the LTTE, by the GOSL and the Muslim community in the north-east. The LTTE shall have an absolute majority on the ISGA for four years. The Muslim and the Sinhala communities in the north-east shall have representatives in the ISGA, but the LTTE will have more than 50 per cent. The chairperson will be elected by a majority vote of the ISGA (which means the LTTE), and serve as chief executive. He shall appoint a chief administrator for the north-east, and all officers. Representatives of the Muslim community have the right to participate in the formulation of their role in the ISGA. But, the Muslims will have to accept the ISGA i.e. permanent subservience to the LTTE; they can only talk about their role in the ISGA. Can the Muslims settle for this lowly status when they already constitute more than 40 per cent of the population of the east?
14. *References to the government of Sri Lanka (GOSL) in the proposal.* The GOSL is mentioned in only ten places in the entire agreement, and always in the context of having to do something, or give up something; never in the context of exercising powers or rights reflecting the sovereignty of the state. The references are the following:
    a) Some members of the ISGA to be appointed by the government.
    b) The ISGA to exercise all powers and functions of the government in the north-east.
    c) The government shall make good faith efforts to implement the recommendation of the ISGA for funds out of the Consolidated Funds.
    d) The proceeds of all grants and loans made by the government to the North-east General Fund shall be under the control of the ISGA.
    e) The armed forces of the government shall immediately vacate all land in the north-east.

f) The government must also compensate owners of such land for past dispossession.

g) The government and the ISGA shall enter into a water use agreement.

h) All proceeds of agreements and contracts under the jurisdiction of the ISGA shall be paid by the government to the ISGA.

i) In the case of any dispute between the parties as to the interpretation or implementation of the agreement, it shall be referred to arbitration consisting of three persons. One by each of the parties; the chairman to be appointed by both parties; and on the failure of agreement, the parties shall request the president of the International Court of Justice to appoint a chairperson

j) In the determination of any such dispute, there shall be parity of status of the LTTE and the government.

The above clauses virtually confer on the LTTE the status of a sovereign entity.

15. *Clause 16. Land Administration*. The proposed Special Commission on Land Administration which is to report on the rights of dispossessed people over land, subject to encroachment, notwithstanding the lapse of any time relating to prescription, puts in jeopardy the rights of impoverished settlers of all communities who were given state grants of land under the then prevailing laws, from a time prior even to Independence. This section is a potential time bomb. The dispossession of long established settlers will cause havoc.

Let me state categorically that, however far reaching the LTTE's proposals are, all the major political parties in Sri Lanka are agreed that negotiations with the LTTE must continue, that the proposals submitted by them must be used as a basis for negotiation, and that the ceasefire must be maintained.

Finally, I venture to suggest that it will soon become necessary for India to consider seriously, I might even use the expression 'face up to', the looming denouement of the ethnic problem in Sri Lanka. On the part of India, a proactive involvement in shaping the solution to our problem will become inescapable. The exertion of such important influence should not be left to other countries outside our region who do not have, and should not be allowed to have, if my conceptual framework stands valid, a permanent stake in our region.

Some questions will arise for India's consideration. What kind of constitutional arrangement in Sri Lanka will India be able to live with? A form of federalism? How close should it be to the Indian Constitution? A confederation of two states in Sri Lanka? Two separate states with no link between them? Can India accept a 'homeland' for the Tamil people? Can India accept the marginalisation of the Muslim community in the east when the Muslim community in India has been integrated into the Indian Union?

"Terrorism has become a real challenge for the whole of humanity ... The final outcome was that people of God were slaughtering people of God in the name of God, and in the House of God. They were slaughtering them by justifying the acts "in the name of Allah the Beneficent and the Merciful." Now, can anyone of sound mind justify that?"

Asfandyar Wali Khan

President, Awami National Party, Pakistan

I am confident that debate and discussions on this forum will go a long way in promoting the process of peaceful dialogue for resolving conflicts in South Asia. This seminar on the peace dividend is taking place at a very significant point of time in our history. The recent confidence building measures, approved by both Pakistan and India have created a new hope for the commencement of a meaningful dialogue between the two countries.

Let us hope that both the countries would not miss this historic opportunity for making a breakthrough in peacefully resolving their outstanding problems. They simply cannot afford to fail, since our alternative is death and destruction on a very large scale and may even go to a nuclear threat. No one of sound mind can opt for such an alternative.

Human beings around the globe have a profound stake in peace. But, the uniquely significant nature of the dividends of peace for the people of South Asia cannot be denied. It is a fact that more than a billion hardworking people of South Asia, with a magnificent civilisation and heritage and abundant natural resources could not translate the last fifty-six years of their political independence into economic prosperity, because of the destructive wars and lack of good neighbourly relations.

During the same period, people in many other parts of the world were able to make impressive strides on the path of social economic development by making better and more sensible use of their energies and their resources.

We believe that political issues can only be resolved through peaceful and meaningful dialogue. If one studies history one finds that no political issue has ever been solved militarily.

Let us go back in history. It is not that India and Pakistan have never been in dialogue. We engaged in dialogue in Tashkent, but only after the deaths and destruction of the 1965 Indo-Pak war. More talks followed in Simla, but it was after the 1971 war. Let us hold discussions *before* the death and destruction of war. As the saying goes, everything that a clever man does, a fool would also do, but after a lot of destruction has taken place.

More than political will, I think the solution lies in political courage, in political perseverance and sincerity. We have no time to waste, since we have a lot of catching up to do in different fields. Our region has suffered gravely due to communal hatred and sectarian strife. Tens of thousands of innocent people have lost their lives in communal conflicts in the twentieth century. As we fail to root out this disease from our social and political fabric, we forget the lessons of non-violence, sectarianism and communal harmony that were taught to us by Mahatma Gandhi, Vinoba Bhave, and Khan Abdul Ghaffar Khan.

And I think that was not enough. We were engulfed by a wave of extreme religious movements in the 1980s, during the Cold War confrontation. This brought in religious extremism.Religious extremism is not an indigenous phenomenon of the Pakhtoons. I want to make that point being a Pakhtoon myself. Religious extremism was injected into Pakhtoon society in the early 1980s. The madrasas are still being funded by the petrodollars of the Middle East. Until these finances of the fundamentalists are controlled, I feel that no power, no government will be able to control fundamentalism. You have to keep in mind that in the end it was this same fundamentalism that turned into international terrorism.

Terrorism has become a real challenge for the whole of humanity, but it has particularly destablised and polarised the whole South Asian region. A perfect example would be the Taliban in Afghanistan. They not only destroyed the basic fabric of society in Afghanistan but also had a profound effect on the whole region. The final outcome was that people of God were slaughtering people of God in the name of God, and in the House of God. They were slaughtering them by justifying the acts "in the name of Allah the Beneficent and the Merciful." Now, can anyone of sound mind justify that?

Our Islam is an Islam of love. Islam is the religion of tolerance. Islam is the religion of forgiveness.

I believe that fortunately, due to the timely rescue of the international community, Afghanistan instead of becoming an Arab colony today, has been returned to the Afghans. I say this because I sincerely believe the Taliban were upfront, and the authority in Afghanistan registered with the Taliban. But the de facto authority in Afghanistan rested with Al-Qaeda. It rested with Osama bin Laden.

My house is about seven or eight kilometres from the Durand Line. We thought the maximum number of Arabs that would be in Afghanistan with Osama bin Laden was 2,000 to 3,000. But, actually there were 24,000 Arabs armed to their teeth! Many of you will remember the fact that, immediately after 9/11, a council of Ulemas collected in Kabul. They asked Taliban leader Mullah Omar to request Osama to leave Afghanistan. If power was in the hands of Mullah Omar, Osama bin Laden would have left Afghanistan.But he did not. Osama challenged that authority, and it is anybody's guess where he is now.

Following the footprints of Khan Abdul Ghaffar Khan, the Awami National Party has consistently taken a strong position against violence in the name of religion, and we have always supported peaceful resolutions of interstate and intrastate conflict. We believe that all those who support peace, harmony, democracy, pluralism, secularism and human rights across the nation, the region, and indeed, across the globe, have to close their ranks for overcoming the banes of extremism and violence.

Regional cooperation on an institutionalised basis is a prerequisite for sustainable speedy and healthy social and economic development. The experience of a number of countries in different regions during the last three or four decades has decisively proved the significance of regional cooperation for economic development. It is also very useful in getting a better deal for the ever-deepening process of globalisation. In fact, problems like environment, drugs, and illegal immigration can't be effectively tackled at the individual level. They can be better addressed on a regional level.

Unfortunately, South Asia lags far behind in developing an effective and systematic regional cooperation. Harmonising relations between India and Pakistan is the solution to making South Asia a peaceful and forward-looking region.

As I pointed out earlier, our party has taken a firm stand on peace, secularism, and peaceful dialogue throughout. We stood by our principles even under circumstances when ours was the lone voice in Pakistan, rising above communal hatred and polarisation. Omar Abdullah, like me, a third generation political worker, also believes in dialogue. We too have been asking for dialogue these last fifty-six years. We have gone to jail time and again. I think after the Field Marshal, there can be no prime minister or martial law administrator, no President of Pakistan in whose period I have not gone to jail. We have always raised our voices for peace, because it is the legacy of Khan Abdul Ghaffar Khan. I feel proud of that legacy.

It is a very heavy burden to carry a legacy like this. We will keep struggling till we have a tension-free brotherly South Asia.

'To realise her full potential, India needs a stable and secure Pakistan. For too long, too many people in India have seen Pakistan as a rival, but in the long run India has to see Pakistan as a partner, since like it or not, features of these countries are intermittently intertwined.'

Richard Haass

President, Council on Foreign Relations, New York

My perspective on South Asia is the perspective of one American. There are four issues that I think cut through the core of security in this part of the world.

The first is obviously the relationship between India and Pakistan, the two most important states in this part of the world. Today there is considerable optimism. I think back two years ago to this month, and it is hard to exaggerate the degree of contact now. And that is obviously welcome, but at the risk of being the proverbial—if I may use an American expression, 'skunk at the garden party'—let me still suggest several reasons why I am not sanguine about the situation in South Asia.

The relationship between India and Pakistan is still a remarkably underdeveloped relationship. It is a relationship that has precious little breadth. It is a relationship that has precious little depth. It is brittle. The comparison I am always drawn to, is that at the height of the Cold War between the United States and the Soviet Union, there was far more going on in far more areas between the United States and the Soviet Union than, there is between India and Pakistan today.

So, while the events of the last two weeks are obviously welcome, I do not think that we should delude ourselves and lose sight of the reality, which again is that this is a fundamentally underdeveloped bilateral relationship.

As welcome as the ceasefire is along the Line of Control and the Siachen glacier, from what I understand nothing has yet been done by the Government of Pakistan to dismantle the camps or the so-called infrastructure of terror that still characterises the situation, and which could be turned on to a greater degree at any moment.

And, in some ways, elaborating on my first point, ceasefires are fine, but ceasefires are not nearly enough. We need a far more extensive dialogue. I look forward to the day when an Indian prime minister travels to Pakistan or vice versa, or foreign ministers or foreign secretaries meet, and this barely makes news. Right now if it happens, it is obviously the lead story.

We may need all sorts of people-to-people contacts. Essentially, at all levels of society, interaction between Indians and Pakistanis has to become a norm rather than the exception. Trade needs to be the dominant link between these two societies, between these two countries. Formal legal trade is miniscule. I don't have the numbers in front of me, but I think there is more trade, say, between the United States and Canada in an afternoon, than there is between India and Pakistan in a year. That simply does not make sense for either country.

Some progress has been made in the area of confidence-building measures, but not nearly enough. Much more also needs to be done to change the tone of the relationship. We want to reach a point where textbooks that young students read, shouldn't perpetuate stereotypes.

One idea, which I think should receive greater focus here, is the idea of building a natural gas pipeline across Pakistan. I like it not simply because it would bring economic benefits to both countries, but we would have created a situation of mutual dependence. India would be to some extent dependent upon the output of the gas. Pakistan would be to some extent dependent upon the regular receipt of revenue out of that mutual dependence.

I welcome the progress of the last two weeks, but I don't think anyone should delude himself that much more remains to be done.

That's only one dimension of the security challenge in South Asia. The second one is Pakistan itself. What we need in Pakistan is the continuation, and ultimately the completion of reform. We need Pakistan to be a functioning democracy. It is not. We need the full return of civilian rule. We need fundamental economic reform, fundamental legal reform, educational reforms, social reforms, civil society and all the rest.

Pakistan really needs to become a modern, functioning complete nation-state with transparent institutions, transparent procedures and accountability of those who wield power.

And until that happens, I would suggest that Pakistan would not necessarily be a good neighbour for India. But more important, forces within Pakistani society will be a threat not simply to Pakistan, not simply to India, but to an entire region and to the world. So, a lot of national construction or to use the favourite phrase, nation-building, still remains to be done in Pakistan, despite the fact that it's more than half a century old.

Thirdly, looking broadly at the task in South Asia today, is the challenge of Afghanistan. Again, it is hard to exaggerate what has happened in the last two years. But again it is also hard to exaggerate what still remains to be done in nation-building there. One really needs to see the extension of central government authority in a meaningful way throughout the entire country. Right now, there is an uneasy balance between the government and President Karzai and the power of what you formalistically called regional authorities, and what is realistically called local authorities.

As you all know, drug production has reached all-time highs. The Taliban, to some extent, is making comebacks in parts of the society. There is still too much violence, too many guns in the wrong hands. The national police, the national military are yet to be in full control. Roads are getting built at an extremely slow rate. The entire challenge of making Afghanistan a modern state is still before us.

Fourth and last, in addition to the bilateral relationship between India and Pakistan, in addition to the situation in Pakistan itself, in addition to Afghanistan, is the goal of making South Asia a region.

Regions have got to be entities that are diplomatic, economic and not simply geographic. The goal ought to be to not only develop a SAARC, but also other institutions to make South Asia a region more than merely a geographic reality. I would think the emphasis in the initial phase should largely be on the economic.

Those who say a fundamentally transformed relationship between India and Pakistan is patriotism, are saying what we said about France and Germany half a century ago. There is a model there that holds out not simply a past, but also lot of inspiration.

I would suggest that, despite the fact that India is the strongest state in South Asia, we need a stable and secure South Asia. The reason is quite simple. If India is not to be distracted, if India is not to see its resources drained—or to put it more positively, if India is to realise its potential, not simply in part of the world, but beyond, in the larger Asia and also globally, India needs stability in South Asia. Otherwise, this part of the world literally becomes the proverbial ball in a chain that precludes India, and prevents India, from realising its full potential.

In order for this to happen though, India needs a stable and secure Pakistan. For too long, too many people in India have seen Pakistan as a rival. But in the long run, India has to see Pakistan as a partner, since like it or not, features of these countries are intertwined.

If Pakistan fails to complete the trajectory that we discussed a few minutes ago, if Pakistan fails to become a modern functioning democracy in every sense of the word, then not simply Pakistanis, but I believe Indians will pay a price as well. And this suggests to me that it is in India's interest to be as generous as it can be towards Pakistan. Not as a favour to Pakistan, but as a favour to itself.

Indeed, to a large extent I believe India's future will in many ways be influenced by Pakistan's future and it is for that reason that I, among others, applaud the sort of initiatives that we have seen from the Prime Minister here. I think that is the sort of visionary approach that India needs to take again, not simply as a goodwill gesture to its neighbour, but as an investment in its own future.

Lastly, and I feel comfortable in saying this, I believe that India and for that matter Pakistan, too partner with the United States. What 9/11 brought home in a very negative way was how American interest and how America's future is intertwined with this part of the world. There are also more positive lessons that have been brought home, and one is the blossoming economic relationship between the United States and India. When one looks at the role of Indian Americans in the United States, when we look at the demographics, when we look at the economic potential and so forth, Americans increasingly see South Asia not simply as a problem but also as an area of tremendous possibility. And it is obviously very much in our interest to see that this possibility be realised.

One of the points made earlier today was that South Asia matters. Yes, obviously South Asia matters. I think the good news now is that Americans understand it, and American foreign policy increasingly reflects the growingly centrality of South Asia, not simply of importance to the United States, but to the world.

Q & A: Securing South Asia

Q: Mr Khan, in your presentation you avoid that 'K' word, Kashmir. In India, people in responsible positions are mentioning the Line of Control as a possible solution to Kashmir. There are voices against and there are voices in favour. Even the Chief Minister of Kashmir said that the LoC solution could be a part of the solution, but not the whole solution. So people in India at least are talking openly about this. I would like to know the position in Pakistan. I know the position of the Chief Executive Officer of Pakistan. But what is the prevailing point of view among the people of Pakistan? Is there any public opinion in Pakistan that talks of a solution other than taking over the entire Valley, the entire Jammu & Kashmir State?

Asfandyar Wali Khan: What we feel is that, whenever you are going for a dialogue, if you go with a certain mindset—you take your mindset and I take my mindset—how do we get together? Where do we get together?

I want my child to live in a better environment than I have lived. Now these are issues when once you sit across the table, let the governments decide.

Both sides have to accept the fact that adjustments have got to be made. Unless both sides are prepared to make adjustments in their stated stands, you cannot find a solution to it. So, I would beg of everyone—never, ever go to a negotiating table with a fixed mindset, because you will then not be able to reach an agreement.

Q: Mr Haass, you mentioned the three E's (economic reform, elected government, educational reform) in Pakistan. Unfortunately

there is a disjunction between this policy option, and your presentation input where you said we need to support President Musharraf. I see that they run in contradiction, because supporting President Musharraf means supporting the establishment of Pakistan. I don't have to remind you of the Musharraf doctrine which was laid out in Karachi on 13 April 1999, when he was the army chief and he said that even if the Kashmir solution is to Pakistan's satisfaction, the low intensity conflict with India will continue. And secondly, that Pakistan will never allow Indian influence. The question is, how do you resolve this disjunction in the points that you have made. Is there any way by which the United States and India can persuasively create a condition by which Pakistan can come to a full blooded democracy at the earliest opportunity, which I am quite certain will contribute towards peace and stability.

Richard Haass: Let me address the second question, with two points. One is, you get out of what I think is one of the toughest foreign policy problems that the United States faces. And it is not unique to Pakistan—it could be Pakistan, it can be Russia. (The problem arises) when you have a number of goals simultaneously. In the case of Pakistan, it is to promote reform, and the restoration of democracy. But, it is also to try to promote a better relationship with India, to offer Pakistani help in the pursuit of terrorism, to go after Al- Qaeda, and one could add several other goals. So the question is, how do you pursue all these goals simultaneously?

It is equivalent to Russia. When Mr Putin does certain things that are, shall we say, anti-democratic, how does one maintain a support vis-à-vis Iran, North Korea, or Iraq?

It is a difficult foreign policy problem (and) that is the one we face with Pakistan. That said, I do think in the long run, we have to make clear our commitment to reform, and the way we just suggested it in our Council for Foreign Relations study. One way is that the United States should provide a percentage of its foreign assistance to Pakistan regardless of what happens. But economic assistance above a certain level, as well as military assistance above a certain level, should be conditioned on certain types of reforms, should be conditioned on the rule of law, and certain types of economic and legal reforms. Because we want to make sure that the aid is going to help bring about the sort of Pakistan we want to see.

Again, we can also use our voice publicly and privately to encourage the sort of Pakistan we want to see. We don't have control over this, but we do have influence over it. And what I simply want to suggest is that, this is one of those classic foreign policy problems, where we need to maintain cooperation in the present, and at the same time try to promote reform over time, so that in the future we see a different country.

Social Virtues

And The Creation

OF PROSPERITY

Francis Fukuyama

'Trust is critical in any society. It is a social capital. It is something that produces well, just as physical capital or human capital produce well — social capital being the ability for people to work together on the basis of trust and a certain kind of social virtue.'

Francis Fukuyama

Professor of International Political Economy at the Paul H. Nitze School of Advanced International Studies, Johns Hopkins University

I am not going to talk about philosophy at all. I am going to talk about some very concrete issues having to do with world order, and I am going to begin with the issue of trust. Then, I am going to go on to international institutions and my analysis of what is going on in the world and how we can move in some ways to fix this.

South Asia is not an area or region of the world that I feel terribly comfortable giving you advice on. There are many people in this room who know much better, but I do want to talk about how trust comes about in international relations that might have some implications here. We are obviously at a very delicate moment in world affairs. There has been a tremendous amount of instability, danger, conflict; a great deal of uncertainty about the future of the world order--particularly in the period since the 9/11 attacks. And there has been, I think, a great need for international institutions to promote trust and cooperation, but those institutions are either lacking, or had been weakened in the course of the last few years.

But there is also a great deal of opportunity, as I think the ceasefire between India and Pakistan indicates. A great deal more institution building needs to be done, so let me go through this step by step.

Let's begin with the general problem of trust. This is something I have written about, and social scientists have considered, because trust is absolutely critical in any society. At a national level, if people do not trust each other, neither politics, nor economy works.

Trust is a kind of lubricant. It is so important for international economy that many economists and other social scientists have talked about it in terms of the concept of social capital. It is a form of capital. It is something that produces well, just as physical capital or human capital produce well—social capital being the ability for people to work together on the basis of trust and a certain kind of social virtue.

There are two sources of trust. One has to do with the formal rules of the contracts, the agreements that are enforceable through a rule of law and hard system. Within a single nation, those are the formal elements of trust. But there is also an informal layer that is, if anything, more crucial, and has to do with the shared values and norms that exist among people within a society. And I don't think it is possible to have trust without both the formal and the informal levels. This is as true at a national level as it is at an international level.

Between states, trust can come about as a result of treaties, and agreements of multilateral organisations and international institutions. Here, we have the problem that there is no sovereign that will enforce those agreements. It is simply a matter of voluntary agreement between sovereign nation states. But there is a formal level of international law. Here again, it is the informal shared values in norms that create the background that makes international cooperation and enhanced international trust possible.

The European Union is probably the single most ambitious effort to create an international multilateral organisation that ultimately will take on the characteristic of a sovereign nation state. It is only possible in Europe, where countries share a common civilisation, a common cultural background, and in the twentieth century, a very similar set of experiences including two world wars, and the conflicts that emerged. It is hard to think of another part of the world that could create this degree of international cooperation without a similar background of shared informal values.

The problem with most other international organisations is that they can't take for granted such a shared normative background. During the Cold War, the United Nations, the premier international organisation was almost completely hobbled from playing any serious security role by the ideological conflict that existed between the Soviet Union and the United States. With the end of the Cold War, there was hope that there would be a greater degree of consensus among countries over principles of human rights and democracy. But, in fact, I would say, that thirteen or fourteen years after the end of the Cold War, there is probably less trust internationally than there was then. So the question is, how did we get into this situation and how do we get out of it?

There are proximate sources of distrust in the world community. And in many ways this is going to focus on the United States, because I think that the US has played an important role in setting the current, somewhat unfortunate, situation in global politics.

There are really three stages to this. There is a big change that came about as a result of the 9/11 attack in terms of the kind of security threats that existed in the world. The second stage is the US reaction to it, the kind of preventive or pre-emptive war doctrine that the US promulgated. And third, the rest of the world's reaction to the first exercise of that doctrine, in the war in Iraq. Let me go through each of these stages.

The 9/11 attack really did create something genuinely new in international relations, which was the combination of weapons of mass destruction with Islamist suicide terrorism. Both these phenomena have existed separately in the world for many years—we are all familiar with both of them. But it is a combination of the two that creates a particular problem for international relations.

It means that a non-state actor who formerly had no way of affecting the great powers in world politics, now has a kind of democratised source of violence which can be applied with very great effect. Of course, this is not what happened on 9/11. Al Qaeda was not using weapons of mass destruction. But the possibility of it was made vivid by the technology used in the destruction. It was high technology of an advanced country against itself, and it is this that creates a problem, because conventional politics, world politics, revolves around nation-states.

We know how to contain nation-states, we know how to deter them. The whole balance of power doctrines that were invented in the nineteenth century and which were applied to the United States and the Soviet Union during the Cold War, all applied to the world nation-state. They don't work terribly well against non-state actors and today it requires a different type of security situation or security arrangement to deal with that.

This leads to the second stage of this sequence of developments arising from 9/11—the American reaction to it. The Bush administration announced a war on terrorism. It enunciated a doctrine that essentially incorporated the kinds of principles that I just outlined, having to do with this new type of threat that did not come from nation-states. It was elaborated in the series of speeches, beginning with President Bush's famous, State of the Union address in January 2002—'Axis of Evil'—and finally in the national security strategy document that the United State published in September 2002. That document is perfectly unobjectionable; it makes the argument that I just made. In a sense, international politics has ended with the presence as well as the potential of WMDs in the hands of terrorists. This is not deterrable or containable through conventional tools of diplomacy and national security.

The problem with the American doctrine is that it was stated in a context that did not give anybody reassurance that there would be limits on the way that the pre-emptive response of that document outlined, would be used. The US argued, President Bush argued—I think quite rightly—that in certain circumstances, pre-emption would have to be part of the tool kit that any power would use in defending itself from this kind of threat. I think that is a point of fact. Although many object to doctrine pre-emption, this is in fact the resort that many countries end up relying on, and certainly this is not new in American foreign policy. President Kennedy during the Cuban missile crisis considered pre-emptions against the Soviet missiles in Europe. Other countries have relied on this kind of thing before. The problem, I think, is that the American option was not put in a context that gave people reassurance that this would not become a routine part of the American national security strategy. In fact, because it was stated against the background of President Bush talking about the 'Axis of Evil' that involved not just Iraq, but Iran and North Korea, that people were led to believe that the United States was about to embark on a series of interventions in pursuit of its war on terrorism.

This is a little bit ironic and I think shows the failure of American diplomacy. I don't believe that the Bush administration actually ever intended to use this particular tool against any other country other than Iraq. But because this was not explained to the world community adequately, people did not have great reason to believe otherwise. Then we have the war in Iraq that became the first test or implementation of the doctrine, with results that you are all familiar with. I think this then, led to the third stage in world politics, which was the global reaction against this new American policy— the rise of a kind of global anti-Americanism, impacting on the United States' old allies, European allies and the NATO alliance.

I frankly find it quite significant since I don't think that this intensity of opposition is something that has really been seen in any of the trans-Atlantic disputes that existed in the period of the Cold War. Now this was the security change that I think led to a high degree of distrust being injected into the international system over the last several years, and the attack on sovereignty.

Implicit in that security doctrine, however, was another set of changes that started long before 9/11, that were working to undermine the general principle of sovereignty within the international system, and that had to with the factor of failed states in world politics. One of the characteristics of the post Cold War world is a band of very weak countries extending from the western Mediterranean through central Asia, to this part of the world, where there are states that either were too weak to govern their populations adequately, or had failed entirely.

This is the single theme that unites the many global order problems, from poverty to drug trafficking, and ultimately, to international terrorism. Over the past fifteen years this has led to a number of international interventions beginning with military force, but leading to a nation-building effort by the international community to try to provide governance that could not be provided locally by the states themselves. It is the failure of governance that really led to the undermining of the principle of sovereignty. This is not something that started with the Bush administration's doctrine of pre-emptive war. It is something that the international community had actually begun to endorse long before.

In other words, people made principled arguments that the old system that assumed or accepted the sovereignty of the de facto power holders in the international system was not adequate, that we could not let a person like Milosevic who had committed crimes against humanity hide behind the nominal sovereignty. What actually went on in the states was intensely important to countries around the world, to the international community—i.e. if they violated human rights, if they produced refugees, if they committed aggression against their neighbours. And all of these tended to go together. The same states tended to produce the same set of outcomes whereby the international community took it upon itself to violate their sovereignty in order to improve governance.

This leads to two general kinds of world order problems. To start with, it sets up two categories of states. It sets up one category of sovereign state, and it sets up another category of state whose sovereignty is violated. It raises an immediate normative question as to who has the right to decide when and where to intervene, and against what forms of injustice, and what kind of human rights violations. The second problem that it raises is the problem of nation-building, which in a way is a more political and technical question, of how the international community actually organises itself to provide good governance for those countries that do not have it.

There have been a greater number of exercises in nation-building since the end of the Cold War than during that period. We have seen this in Panama and Cambodia, Somalia, Haiti, Rwanda, Congo, Bosnia, Kosovo, and East Timor. Afghanistan and Iraq are the most recent. I think that what we have to conclude from this experience is that neither the United States nor other members of the international community, including the United Nations, actually knows how to do this terribly well.

I think the international community is reasonably good at providing post conflict stabilisation, and reconstruction and humanitarian assistance. In places like Bosnia, following the accord, this was relatively poorly organised, but nonetheless it was effectively done. The real problem that the international community does not have a good mechanism for dealing with, is that of creating self-sustaining government institutions that allow failed states—or poorly governed or badly governed states—to stand on their own without the assistance and support of the international community. It is really that sort of thing that you see today in Bosnia. Seven years after the conclusion of the accord with the strong presence of international peacekeepers, of international police, and high levels of economic assistance, you still have a situation in which there is basically no self-governance in Bosnia. The high representative has been compared by a couple of recent writers to a European rogue, in the sense that the high representative can overturn an election, can overturn officials in that country on grounds of corruption charges, or for other reasons. I think everyone would admit that without the presence of the international community, it is quite likely that Bosnia will slide back into the kind of chaos that led to the intervention in the first place. So the problem or the craft of creating self-sustaining institutions, state institutions to do real nation-building that would facilitate an exit by the international community, has not been overcome.

One interesting dimension of this has been revealed by the different reactions to the Iraq war and to American foreign policy. A different concept of legitimacy led to the question of who has the right to make decisions to intervene, whether on behalf of human rights, or to protect a nation from security threats from international terrorism. Here, there are big differences revealed between Americans and Europeans in particular, that have been at the root of some of the psychological problems and the distrust in the international community.

The United States has a very different sense of the source of international legitimacy. It believes that the ultimate source of legitimacy is a constitutionally ordered democratic decision on the part of a sovereign democratic nation. And that international legitimacy does not exist on its own, but only to the extent that it is handed up from democratically constituted governments to an international organisation. This is quite different from the European concept which holds that there is international legitimacy which exists apart from the wishes of democratic majorities and individual nation-states, and that those are embodied in international institutions handed downwards.

There is exceptionalism on both sides. The United States has always had a sense of the exceptional quality of its own democratic institutions that it regarded as a universal model for other societies around the world. There is a degree of European exceptionalism because Europe is a part of a world in the process of trying to transcend national sovereignty handed off, in fact, to a super-national organisation. I would say that India and China have a different history, somewhere in between and probably more respectful than the United States, of the legitimacy of the United Nations. But, on the other hand, given India's past colonial history, and given the relationship that it has had with others, it is much more defensive of its national sovereignty. This is something, that is changing.

If this is the problem of the world order, if this is why we have international distrust, the obvious solution to gaining international trust is, through more authentic international institutions. That would normally be both a way of addressing the security problem and a way of nation-building, or international governance that is so critical. In fact, many people have turned to the United Nations as a source of help on both of these questions.

I believe that the United Nations is an important source of legitimacy. It does play an extremely important role, especially in nation-building exercises around the world. However, it has some major problems with both legitimacy and effectiveness which in certain ways are not flexible, limiting its role in world politics. This will prevent it from helping the problems that the world is facing.

Let me deal with the legitimacy problem. The whole concept of world government or world federalism can be traced back to the great German philosopher, Emmanuel Kant and his essay on perpetual peace. Here he first suggested the idea of a League of Nations, a concept that emerged from World War I, and the United Nations, which followed World War II. However, Kant did not actually propose an institution that looked like the present day United Nations. He stipulated that such an organisation would have to be based on the union of states that had a republican form of government. In other words, those that were liberal democracies in some form. And the reason for that is the issue of trust that I mention earlier.

Without a fundamental consensus on the values that underpin legitimate governance, it would be impossible for this kind of League of Nations to have a sufficient degree of consensus and really be able to solve any kind of serious security or other problems, involving normative judgments. The United Nations by contrast is not based on any kind of substantive principle of legitimacy. It is based on a mere principle of sovereignty; it is, of course, a recognition of de facto power holders without asking how they got their power, and whether that power is democratically legitimate. This leads to problems like the current one in the United Nations were Libya is currently the chairman of its Human Rights Commission.

The problem of its effectiveness is a more practical one. The Security Council, supposed to deal with world order, was deliberately designed by the founders of the United Nations to be a weak institution. It gave a special role, a permanent veto to the five victors of World War II thereby permitting them to prevent the Security Council from ever contradicting the fundamental security interests of those five shareholders. As a result, the requirement for unanimous consensus has meant that the United Nations is not affected when the most severe kinds of security problems affect its own members. I know that there have been quite a number of proposals to address this problem over the last few years. I do not believe that this is feasible because with every alternative order the Security Council raises, it creates winners and losers that basically have a veto over the reform process itself. It is something that cannot be overcome. So, if India were to be a member of the Security Council, Pakistan would object; if Japan were to be made a member, other Asian countries would not like it; if the European Union were to occupy British and French seats, neither Britain or France would accept that outcome.

On the other hand, the current American approach to security, to rely not on existing well-established international or multilateral organisations, but to rely instead on coalitions of the willing, is not a solution either. Coalitions of the willing is simply a fig leaf on US unilateralism. It may be effective militarily in a narrow sense by being able to put together a group of countries that can win the active combat phase of the war as we saw in Iraq, but it doesn't provide the kind of legitimacy to action that allows them the formation of a broader international coalition and greater international cooperation. The problems that the United States has got into in Iraq are good examples of the narrowness of vision with which it entered the war, and the subsequent problems. How can one go forward when there are impediments in the inherent mechanism of a recognised international nation-building institution?

Institutions and mechanisms that will improve international trust need two things. They need power, and they need legitimacy. We should not underestimate the power aspect. There has been much criticism of the Bush administration assertions that military force can actually bring about democratic outcomes. But let us remember what happened in the Balkans, in the 1990s. The Europeans with their soft power were unable to get to the fundamental cause and instability in the Balkans—which was Serbia—and the policies undertaken by President Milosevic. It was really only the Croat and ultimately, NATO air power, that tilted the balance of power in that region and got rid of Milosevic, and led the way to the ceasefires in both Bosnia and Kosovo. Legitimacy is also crucial to solving these problems. Power without legitimacy can be undermined, and therefore, we need institutions that are able to carry this out.

We need a multiplication of institutions around the world with overlapping mandates and memberships. In a way, this is what we already have though not as a deliberate effort towards international security. The more international and regional institutions we have, the better off we are, because there would be at least one institution that will be appropriate for any given particular kind of conflict. An example is Kosovo, where the Russian veto made it impossible to use the Security Council to authorise intervention against Serbia. So, NATO was asked to intervene. There are a number of other new institutions where creativity could increase their strength and effectiveness.

When Madeleine Albright was Secretary of State of the United

States, she helped found a community of democracies that, like the NATO alliance, was based on democratic practice. This community of countries that share democratic principles, could, if developed further, become an alternative source for the legitimisation of international action in support of goals that we plan to favour, such as promotion of democracy and human rights.

Finally, we need to think seriously about architectures for Asian regional cooperation in a larger context, rather than bilateral relationships that have dominated the politics here. There is a deficit of international, and particularly, of multilateral institutions in this part of the world. I think the reason is the contrast with Europe. There is a lack of a framework of shared values encompassing a much greater diversity in religions, cultures and historical traditions in Asia and South Asia. It is a region where the economically most dominant and powerful country, Japan, is still highly distrusted by its immediate neighbours Korea and China. This has made the formation of larger and stronger kinds of multilateral organisations impossible, although some, like ASEAN, exist. Most security arrangements tend to be bilateral—the US treaties with South Korea, Japan, the Philippines, or the Chinese-Pakistani relationship, or the old relationship that the former Soviet Union held with India, with Vietnam, with North Korea and the like.

This is an insufficient basis for Asian security. There is an opportunity to move beyond bilateral arrangements to a broader form of multi-lateralism. China is thinking along these lines. I make no brief for Chinese foreign policy, but interesting things have been going on in that country over the past decade. The Chinese have progressed from seeing themselves as outsiders and victims of the international system with a lot of grievances, to a view that they need to ride to being full and equal participants that can shape the international order, whose opinion is respected and whose proposals can be taken seriously by other members of the international community. They have executed a kind of Neo-Bismarckian policy, because they are very worried about the negative reaction to their growing economic power. This has made them try to suggest various diplomatic and economic proposals to soften any opposition.

They have settled a number of border disputes. They have even had some productive talks with India, with a number of central Asian countries, and have settled some border disputes on terms that are not particularly favourable to them. They have taken a much more active role in the United Nations. They used to abstain from voting for resolutions, e.g. Security Council Resolution 1441 that authorised the return of weapons inspectors to Iraq, because they didn't like the idea of violating another country's sovereignty. But they were full participants in that discussion and actually played quite a useful role as well as in Resolution 1511 — on the transition to Iraqi sovereignty. They have made a whole series of proposals for economic free trade areas, which they argue will be the basis for multilateral security arrangements in the future. They have proposed the China ASEAN free trade areas and ASEAN-plus-three format and ASEAN-plus-one format. In North-east Asia, the free trade area they have laid out is actually a grand vision for an East Asian free trade area ten to fifteen years hence, that would unite all these different sub-regional groupings.

I don't pretend to know what Chinese motivations are. I think both India and Japan take a dark view. They believe that this is a geo-economic strategy that is intended to blunt opposition to growing Chinese economic and ultimately, military, power. But, I think, we have to be also open to the possibility that it marks a kind of shift in Chinese priorities and a maturing of Chinese foreign policy. It has produced an interesting effect. It is stimulating both India and Japan into making competing proposals for other free areas. Japan, for example, has proposed a Japan-ASEAN comprehensive economic partnership; it has negotiated a free trade with Singapore and the like. This is actually a good thing. It is much better for countries to be competing in the sphere of creating new multilateral institutions, than to be competing in the area of military prowess. It is this kind of competition in institution-building that will ultimately lay the basis for a much stronger set of multilateral institutions that will ramify through the whole area.

Trust alone cannot come about simply through the formal creation of these institutions. Democracy is absolutely critical, and countries will not trust China as long as it is run by an authoritarian communist party. Domestic change must accompany foreign policy initiatives. All this has important implications for India, because India, like China, is going through a similar kind of evolution.

India no longer sees itself simply as a victim of the international system and an outsider. It wants to be recognised increasingly as a sole and equal player in that system. One other thing that a full and equal player does, is it provide things like global public goods; it helps in the creation of broader institutions; and provides some of the backbone and the support for bigger public spaces that are ultimately the sources of trust in the international system.

Q & A: Francis Fukuyama

Q: Trust means consistency in action. The US has not been consistent in a lot of its relations. How do you account for that? As for your book *The End of History* do you still believe in that, now that the society is changing?

Francis Fukuyama: Before I came to Delhi, I gave a talk in Italy. After the talk, someone asked me if there is ever a talk where I am not asked about *The End of History*, and whether I think it is still valid or not. But I am perfectly happy to answer that.

Let me begin with the question about US foreign policy. As should be evident from what I said about the behaviour of the Bush administration, there has been a great deal of inconsistency in the application of the idealist side of American foreign policy, and the United States has found itself having to compromise on those principles for security purposes. During the Cold War, we obviously made alliances with a number of authoritarian countries in pursuit of strategic objectives, and I think that has undercut, to some extent, the legitimacy of American behaviour.

I think one of the unfortunate consequences of declaring a war on terrorism is that it has aligned the United States with a lot of other not very democratic countries that are also waging wars on terrorism. And again, Pakistan under General Musharraf is just one example of that. I think that is a problem. It is one, however, that I do not think vitiates the Wilsonian thrust in American foreign policy. There has nonetheless been a strong degree of support in the long run, in a multitude of ways, for the principle of democracy around the world. It just needs to be exercised more consistently.

On the question of *The End of History*, it was an argument about the long-term evolution of human societies as they go from hunter-gatherer to agricultural to industrial, and ultimately, to post-industrial societies. And what I was trying to argue was that evolution was a coherent one and it was one that had political consequences. And that, as countries developed economically, they tended to develop democratic political institutions because you had a middle class, you had people with private properties that needed to be protected, you had higher degrees of education and the like. And I think that whatever has happened in the short run over the last few years, longer term scenarios still very much remain in place.

Samuel Huntington who, incidentally, was my former teacher and remains a friend, would argue something quite different. He would argue that we are not all evolving in the same direction; we are actually going off in different culturally determined directions. I happen to think that is really not the case. There is still a great deal obviously of cultural variance, but I think that there are also certain functional needs that societies have, that lead them to develop similar forms of government. It is my expectation that when China reaches a level of about US$6,000 in per capita GDP, it is probably likely that you will see it to have some kind of a democratic government in place of the current communist authoritarianism. And I think this applies to the Muslim world as well; the experience of Iranians with a generation of misrule by a medieval theocracy has proven to them that they actually want a greater degree of freedom and I would suspect that whatever their cultural beginning points, they are going to want a similar form of government. It will obviously be different in the execution and the implementation but the general aspirations to live in free societies are not going to be different in that Muslim country than in other parts of the world.

Q: You have advocated the right of pre-emptive attacks. It means that you are advocating that powerful countries attack poor and weak countries. Aren't you advocating international terrorism?

Francis Fukuyama: **Well, no! I was trying to explain that, in fact, the pre-emptive doctrine that was enunciated by the Bush administration was actually something that ought to be very rare.**

And that the way it was stated in fact created exactly that impression that they believe that this was somehow right in principle.

I think that it is actually a terrible principle of international relations, and if India, or Russia or China were to promulgate a similar kind of doctrine of pre-emptive war, the United States would be very unhappy with it. So no, it is not a good general principle. And I think the United States made a very big mistake in not fully enunciating the limits of this kind of a doctrine.

What I was trying to say was that, if you are faced with a situation of terrorists armed with weapons of mass destruction that were not part of a nation-state, you had almost no choice but to go after them pre-emptively. Most nations around the world do that sort of thing in their anti-terrorist campaigns, including this country. That's quite different from the kind of major operation that happened in Iraq, which I think is much more grave and needs to be done carefully. But certainly, it is not possible to rule out the need for pre-emption in certain cases.

Q: Today a lot of countries look at the United States with suspicion and scepticism and even hatred because of American foreign policy. Since you spoke about Samuel Huntington, do you really believe that in some ways American foreign policy as it is designed today may in fact create a kind of clash of civilisations? And, does anti-Americanism ever matter to American foreign policy? Is it beginning to matter at all now that the war in Iraq isn't going that well?

Francis Fukuyama: I was not a big fan of the Bush administration's approach to Iraq because it seemed to me that it was an excessive response to a real problem, and that has managed to, in my view, justifiably in many cases trigger a great deal of anti-Americanism around the world. The administration was really very ham-handed in trying to explain itself, but you know, there was a deeper problem involved in its wanting to carry out the war with Iraq.

I was not in favour of this war. I thought that one of the reasons the war would be counterproductive was precisely that you are going to escalate what was war against a relatively small extremist group of Muslim terrorists, into something that would, by all appearances, be like a clash of civilisations. And, that the object of American foreign policy really ought to be to avoid that, by whatever means.

What is left is really to figure out how to get out of this. And I think one consequence of the war having gone badly in the reconstruction phase, is that the United States is actually much more inclined now to go back to the United Nations, to go back to the international community for help. It will probably be a while before people accept that turn as anything but instrumental, so there is a lot of rebuilding of trust that needs to happen.

Q: What would be the ways of producing trust between India and Pakistan, considering that the two countries have had very different levels of successes in political, economic and military arenas? How do you develop trust between two countries when one is successful, and the other much less successful?

Francis Fukuyama: I don't have a lot specific of suggestions beyond the kind of things that have been mentioned by other people, more expert, around the room. But, I suggest that you really need to take this out of the bilateral context.

The improvement in the relationship has to start bilaterally. But actually, broader regional and multilateral institutions will form the larger backdrop for both economic growth, and ultimately, for a greater kind of international cooperation on security issues. And so, when you think about the long-term strategy for dealing with India and Pakistan, it has to be encased not just in the bilateral. Or in other words, the bilateral relationship needs to be encased in an overlapping set of multilateral relations.

For example, a growing free trade area that begins, let us say, between China and South-east Asia, or India and other parts of South-east Asia, should be seen as a kind of magnet that will draw more and more countries in—including, under the right circumstances, Pakistan. That provides an extra incentive for economic reform, just as membership in the EU has been used as a major way of forcing would-be member countries to engage in internal reform.

I don't think there is an easy solution to this. A lot of the problems are internal to Pakistan, and, as I indicated when I talked about nation-building, it is not an easy set of problems to solve. But I do think that if you think about a larger multilateral context, it will provide a certain magnet for promulgating good governance and good economic policy in larger parts of the region.

Keynote Address

Benazir Bhutto

> The peace dividend can be the traditional guns for butter trade-off. In the longer term, a peace dividend is defined by investment ... I am surprised at how our nations see progress on trade as a favour to the other country. I see it as a benefit to the common man in each of our countries.

Benazir Bhutto

Former Prime Minister of Pakistan

I thought hard about whether to accept the gracious invitation to speak at this conference. The politics of a former prime minister of Pakistan—and the leader of Pakistan's most popular party—travelling to India to discuss bilateral relations between our two countries were truly complex.

I believe the threat of a conflict in South Asia ending up in the first nuclear war since Hiroshima is real. Such a conflict could annihilate hundreds of millions without distinguishing whether they were Pakistanis, Indians or Kashmiris. The determination to make a contribution to avoid this nuclear nightmare far outweighed other arguments that could have crossed my mind.

We meet today in a world which is more dangerous and different than we imagined when the Cold War ended, when the Berlin Wall fell. The end of the Cold War promised to herald an era of global peace. The principles of freedom and free markets promised to shake up sluggish economies, and the prospect of a peace dividend was before us.

It was not to be. The world is at war, not peace.

The US led coalition occupies a major Islamic nation that is suffering daily attacks and many casualties. No one knows whether Iraq will survive the present phase.

Both India and Pakistan are under pressure to send troops to Iraq. And both are considering that option separately. How much better it would be if countries in the South Asian region could consult each other on such important measures before taking a final decision!

As I talk to you, the resurgent Taliban are mounting fresh attacks on the Karzai government in Afghanistan. They are mounting attacks against the coalition forces and the NGOs working there.

In Jammu and Kashmir, despite the present welcome ceasefire at the Line of Control, the intensity of violence has yet to decrease.

We must ask ourselves: are we to condemn our future generations to a world of violence, of conflict, of bloodshed? Or war, blood and destruction?

This conference, organised to explore peace initiatives, is an important step in building a different kind of world. A world peace and harmony that can protect the life, liberty and livelihood of every individual irrespective of their race, religion, gender or political affiliation.This is an important responsibility on the leadership of South Asia. This responsibility is all the more grave as the world is involved in the war against terrorism.

Few nations or regions have been spared. Christian churches and Muslim masjids were targets of suicide bombers in Pakistan. Your own parliament became the target of a terrorism attack. Great Britain is a target. Saudi Arabia is a target. Turkey is a target. Indonesia is a target, Australia is a target. The world is threatened with carnage in many corners.

We owe it to ourselves and to our people, to all of South Asia, to make every effort to strive, to seek, to pursue peaceful means for the resolution of the outstanding disputes, for confidence-building and reduction of tension in our region. This is the role I believe we can play together in helping the whole world community deal with the threat of terrorism.

The Pakistan Peoples Party (PPP) which I lead, welcomed Islamabad's announcement of a unilateral ceasefire along the Line of Control, inclusive of Siachen. This measure was taken in response to Prime Minister Vajpayee's twelve-point package of confidence-building measures.

There are those who believe that in the context of Indo-Pak relations, tension can only be reduced when both countries, India and Pakistan, are truly democracies. Of course, yours is a democracy and mine has still to achieve that status.

I believe that democracies do not go to war against other democracies. I say this on the basis of India and Pakistan's history. Since independence, the three wars that took place between India and Pakistan took place under military dictatorships. And since the destabilisation of the democratic government that I led in 1996, Pakistan and India have thrice come close to war.

As a witness to the Simla Agreement, the agreement which prevented full-fledged war between our two countries since 1971, my party and I are committed to the peace process between our countries. It is this commitment, which led the PPP and myself to welcome peace talks between New Delhi and Islamabad, despite the military dictatorship in my country.

We believe that the military rulers' statements for normalisation of relations must be put to the test. If it is false, they will be exposed before the bar of public opinion. And if it is true, the benefit will go to the region.

I believe therefore, it is important to communicate, to enter into dialogue and to test the intentions of each other.

It is to the credit of Prime Minister Vajpayee that he did not lose heart despite the undermining of 'bus diplomacy' and the failure of the Agra Summit. But then Prime Minister Vajpayee is a man of many surprises.

For the time being, the Indo-Pak ceasefire has brought happiness and immediate relief on both sides of the Line of Control. Hundreds of villages with thousands of peoples are worst hit during a military standoff. Mines are laid, maiming many. Constant firing denies villagers sustenance.

The atmosphere of congeniality has increased with the news that Prime Minister Vajpayee is to attend the forthcoming SAARC Summit in Islamabad in January 2004. So a new year begins with new hopes and expectations. The major impact of this ceasefire relates to the Siachen area. Both India and Pakistan spend enormous amounts on maintaining their standoff on this highest and coldest of battlegrounds.

As prime minister, I have travelled twice to the highest peaks of the Siachen glacier, I have been able to see from one glacier to the other, and the two troops that face each other. I have seen the transformation of the glaciers into formidable military camps. Estimates claim that the cost to both countries since 1985 is in the region of roughly twenty billion rupees annually. This huge amount is being spent to sustain and counter each other's confrontation in the icy peaks, against the backdrop of a vast majority of our population that lives under US$2 a day, below the poverty line. The cost in lives, particularly during the Kargil fighting but also otherwise, and to those falling victim to cold-induced injuries is immeasurable.

The announcement of the ceasefire serves as a deterrent to militancy. It minimises the build up of a situation similar to one last year, that could have erupted into massive doom and destruction.

The United States, China and others have welcomed the much-needed ceasefire in the hope that it will create conditions speeding up the peace process. Significantly, the ceasefire has been widely accepted in India and Pakistan, igniting the hope that saner leadership will emerge to overcome the Gordian knot of the Kashmir obstacle.

Prime Minister Vajpayee has indicated that his upcoming visit to Islamabad will include meetings with "everyone". I asked him yesterday if we could assume that "everyone" includes Chief Executive General Musharraf, but Prime Minister Vajpayee was not giving away any secret. He simply smiled. But this indicates to us that if the prime minister has to meet everyone, then is certainly a possibility that he will also meet General Musharraf.

The support for the ceasefire rightly came from the Pakistan Peoples Party, the only federal and broad-based political party in Pakistan outside those created by the establishment. The PPP has the singular honour of making a breakthrough on Siachen during Indo-Pak talks in 1989. It is the architect of the policy of soft borders on the disputed territories enunciated in 1999.

The PPP hopes that the ceasefire plan will be followed by greater travel links between the two countries as well as talks on how to lessen violence and the use of force in the area. The PPP hopes that another ceasefire with militants and the Indian Army can be reached as it was previously reached earlier during Prime Minister Vajpayee's tenure. The lessening of violence in the Valley can be calibrated to the reduction of Indian troops in the area giving a greater sense of security to the Kashmiri people as well as bolstering Indo-Pak relations.

While the borders were silent as the signs of a spring in relations dawned, militants tried to mar the spirit within India-controlled Kashmir. But New Delhi did not make these violent incidents a reason to reject the ceasefire, and this is a positive signal on behalf of New Delhi, to which Islamabad needs to react.

The frequent military standoffs contribute immensely to the poverty in the region. The nuclear detonations of 1998 were a powerful signal to awaken to new realities, which changed the nature of a possible future Indo-Pak war.

As a consequence, public opinion in both countries was building up. Exchanges and visits by parliamentarians, intellectuals and women groups took place. These visits indicated that public opinion was dissatisfied with the festering confrontation, the exchange of fire and the disruption of the normalisation process. The renewed contacts between India and Pakistan are taking place against the backdrop of statements by key officials and politicians, and they have raised New Delhi's concern with General Musharraf. According to these high-level officials in President Bush's office and Tony Blair's, General Musharraf has assured them that he will stop cross-border military activity.

This is a new strategic reality. It is arising out of the ashes of the twin towers that were brought down by the events of 9/11.

Even as the world witnesses the emergence of a post 9/11 world with a zero tolerance for acts of violence, we must be ever vigilant for elements that would do their best to break the prospects of peace. These elements are the militants. They believe that without violence there will be no solution to the settlement of the Jammu and Kashmir issue. During their talks in Islamabad in January, the Indo-Pak leadership will need to discuss how to have borders that are soft and which are also safe from the threat of militant activity.

In war games and scenarios played out by think tanks, fictitious volunteers are seen as the Achilles heels of the normalisation process. These war games have led security agencies to conclude that our region is "one of the most dangerous places on earth." The worry is that a militant could spark a war that neither country really wants. For example, a dramatic attack, similar to the one on the Indian parliament, could create intense public pressure on New Delhi to retaliate against Pakistan, a measure that could trigger war.

Perhaps this is why on the eve of Prime Minister Vajpayee's visit, Islamabad banned some militant groups, froze their accounts and sealed their offices. It is hoped that such groups would not resurface once again when the snows of winter melt.

I take this opportunity to commend the All Parties Hurriyat Conference (APHC). Despite recent divisions, the APHC has kept the doors of dialogue open and the channel with New Delhi active. APHC has an important role to play in facilitating peaceful conditions in Srinagar, as indeed in Muzzafarabad, where parties are also part of the APHC.

In the past, New Delhi extended an invitation for unconditional dialogue to the APHC. Such measures were innovative steps that gave momentum to the search for a solution that could end the threat of conflict from this ancient civilisation. It is tragic that our civilisation, our subcontinent, so full of history and so rich in culture, so full of diversity and populated with a hardworking and talented peoples has remained for so long the most likely site for a nuclear exchange on our planet.

South Asia must begin its search for a peace dividend. The peace dividend can be the traditional guns for butter trade-off. In the longer term, a peace dividend is defined by investment. We must invest in technology. We must invest in infrastructure. We must invest in human capital—specifically on education and health.

Scholars expect peace to break down poverty. A Harvard professor has written in *The Wealth and Poverty of Nations*, that "poverty is inextricably linked to armed conflict." Poverty creates an atmosphere that encourages war for the purposes of national identification, national mobilisation, and as a distraction from social inequality. Fighting poverty was a challenge in Pakistan with one of the highest population growth rates when I took office in 1988.

As prime minister, I demonstrated with Prime Minister Rajiv Gandhi that men and women of goodwill, in both our countries could make fundamental progress.

The nuclear confidence-building treaty that we signed in 1988, a treaty by which we committed not to attack our respective nuclear facilities, was the most important peace accord between us since the Simla agreements signed by our parents in 1972. I am also proud that we were able to establish, for the first time, hotlines between the general headquarters of both our countries, modelled on the hotline between Washington and the Kremlin.

We believed that these confidence-building measures were an important prelude to moving along the cause of peace and in facing the challenge of differing perceptions on the issues of Jammu and Kashmir. We feel strongly on this issue, on both our sides.

Let us not be afraid to have two differing points of view on this outstanding issue before us today. China and India have a border dispute but they do not threaten each other with war. In fact, relations between the two countries keep improving. There are many countries with disputes and disagreements. Yet they manage their affairs in a way that enables their people to know each other through trade, travel and tourism. They share warm relations without prejudice to their differing perceptions.

We can learn from such models of conflict management. We can make a meaningful attempt at resolution and reconciliation in South Asia to truly make progress across the board. And if we do make progress, the dividend before us is compelling.

Immediately after independence, India was Pakistan's most important trading partner. In the early years, 56 per cent of Pakistan's total exports went direct to the Indian market. Thirty-two per cent of our imports came from India. Lahore and Amritsar were important economic hubs where trade flourished with a free flow of goods and services. Then, as our political relations deteriorated in the 1950s, trade trickled away for fifty years.

As the prime minister who proposed a South Asian Tariff Agreement during the Islamabad Summit of 1988 and ratified the SAPTA agreement during her second tenure, I am surprised at how our nations see progress on trade as a favour to the other country. I see it as a benefit to the common man in each of our countries.

Some suggest that the benefits of Indo-Pak trading could be as much as US$14 billion annually. The greatest economic benefit of Indo-Pak trade could occur in the sphere of energy cooperation. India is a rapidly growing energy market able to absorb new sources of supply as they make their work materialise in the region. Pakistan's possible role is in fulfilling this need both as supplier and as a transit route from Iran and Central Asia. This requires construction of pipelines, a major capital investment that can come only when there are guarantees of normalisation on both sides.

I suggest that expanding trade be a useful adjunct to the political process, instead of being constrained by it.

Trade is but one of a great many benefits that peace could bring to the subcontinent. Despite a growing middle class in both countries, the depth of poverty of our underclass mars our image. People from India and Pakistan go to America in search of the American Dream. They feel they have opportunities there to succeed that do not exist in this part of the world. We can offer our people the opportunity of an Asian dream, of a South Asian dream. I dream of a time when our children's lives will be free of self-imposed limitations.

The French philosopher Rousseau said that we were all born free. Yet our societies, cultures, politics, militaries, keep our people chained to illiteracy, ignorance, intolerance, infant mortality, malnutrition and disease. It is time to break free of those chains.

India and Pakistan are nuclear powers. Despite the new cease-fire we glare at each other across the LoC. This is the time to actually move forward as the new year in this new century approaches.

I commend the *Hindustan Times* for organising this high-powered conference. This is a conference that brings together political leaders, international diplomats, scholars, intellectuals and leading voices from the media. It is a conference that involves civil debate.

It is my hope that a leading Pakistani daily will follow the precedent set by the *Hindustan Times* in organising a similar leadership initative in Pakistan. I thank the *Hindustan Times* for bringing together a galaxy of leaders to speak on one of the most important issues of our times impacting on the future one-fifth of humanity. And when a conference takes place in Pakistan, I hope I will be able to attend, as I did here. For currently, I am an exile. I am banned from my country. I am banned from contesting for the premiership of my country, banned from contesting even as a backbencher, banned from seeing my husband who is in the eighth year of his imprisonment, banned from entering my ancestral homes, banned from praying at the graves of my father and my brothers.

I do not despair. In life, an individual make choices. I made mine on the last day of my father's life in a prison that our colonial masters built in the city of Rawalpindi. That was the choice to fight for peace and democracy, to fight for human dignity that must come when people combat hunger, poverty and illiteracy.

I know that realities change. That a person can go from prime minister to prisoner and from prisoner to prime minister. I have seen power from the time that I was a child, and I must tell you that the sense of satisfaction and joy that I felt never came from the chandeliered halls or the turbaned staff, or the pomp and power of governing a state. It came from small acts. It came from giving a child polio drops knowing these small drops would change its life forever. It came from inaugurating a school, providing electricity and water to places that had none. It came from seeing the smile on the faces of a boy or girl who got a job.

The wheel of history turns. There was a time when Prime Minister Gujral could not visit the city he was born in, Jhelum, because our two countries were at cross purposes. Now he, though an Indian can visit Jhelum, and I, though a Pakistani cannot visit my Larkana.

The wheel of history turns. And it turns not just for individuals but for nations. And as the wheel of history turns for the children of Partition, I hope we bequeath to them a better future than our own bitter past.

I conclude with a quote from Alexander Pope, which I used during my last visit to New Delhi two years ago. He said,

"What war could ravish,
Commerce could bestow
And he returned a friend
Who was a foe."

Q & A: Benazir Bhutto

Q: There were two major decisions you took when you were prime minister, which had a major impact on the stability in the region and the world. The first one was in the late 1980s when you hyped the Kashmir problem. Some of your statements were shrill and they motivated a lot of infiltrators and others to come into Kashmir. The second decision you took was I think in 1993 when under your prime ministership, the Taliban issue was raised. What do think of those two decisions now? I would also like to know if the motivation was more military, less political, or was it more political and less military?

Benazir Bhutto: It's quite true that during my first tenure, the Kashmir issue was hyped and it could have motivated the forces, which could perhaps to some extent—although I would not fully agree—be part of the current problem. *That* decision was a joint political and military decision.

There was a view that a low-scale intensity in Kashmir would focus attention on it and lead to its resolution. I would say that there were marked differences between the handling of the Kashmir issue during my two tenures as prime minister and others who ruled Pakistan during that time. During my two tenures the violence in Kashmir remained limited in intensity and (limited) to the Valley. There were to my knowledge, few attacks on civilians, and women and children, and targets were usually military personnel operating there. There were no attacks outside the Valley of Kashmir.

And now I consider this something that is troublesome and would be worrisome to the Indian leadership. And I would say that in contrast, troubles and worries increased when there was change in the leadership of Pakistan because the intensity of violence in the Valley increased. Women and children were also attacked. Both Bombay blasts, during my first stint in the Opposition, and the attack on the Indian Parliament, during my second stint in the Opposition, were outside the disputed area.

I am saying this for the sake of records because I have been asked a direct question about it. But my party has taken a review of how we wish to conduct our relations with India after the nuclear detonations of 1998. We believe that those nuclear detonations place a new factor in calculations of what a low intensity conflict in Kashmir could culminate into unwittingly. And we believe that accidentally triggering a nuclear war would be too dangerous. And since 1998, having reviewed our policy on Kashmir, we in the Pakistan Peoples Party have decided to go back to the Simla agreement, which we believe is the most durable agreement, and we have decided that we cannot allow anything to mar the relations between India and Pakistan.

We have also decided to follow what was proposed by (Indian) Foreign Secretary J.N. Dixit in Cyprus in 1993. We have decided now to follow that proposal to keep Kashmir a separate agenda from Indo-Pak relations, and not to allow progress on one item to preclude lack of progress on other items. We can see that, our perception being as wide as possible on one item can lead to a breakdown in relations, and we don't want that. We want to see progress on commonality of issues which we believe increases trade and cooperation. We will attempt to see how we can replicate that model of the European Union in the countries that constitute the South Asian Association of Regional Cooperation.

Of course, we understand that if there is continuation of violence there will be very little progress on trade or cooperation. There was the challenge in 1998 when we reviewed our foreign policy on India, and then there was 9/11, when we took the second review of our relations with India. Following the events of 9/11 we came to the conclusion that not only will there be a danger of a nuclear holocaust in South Asia, but that the threat of terrorism could define relations in the world community for perhaps the next half century, just as communism was considered a threat for half a century. And in a world environment where there is total lack of tolerance for acts of violence, we decided that it was even more important to change the equations of Indo-Pak relations.

This is why, in November 2001 when I was in India and giving an interview to Vir Sanghvi, I called upon Islamabad to ban militant troops like Lashkar-e-Tayyaba, to prevent them for taking our foreign policies hostage. I was bitterly criticised for doing so, but I have seen that public opinion was on my side. And subsequently, General Musharraf himself banned those groups. They resurfaced, and he has banned them again. Ultimately I believe General Musharraf is acknowledging—or I would hope he is acknowledging, for I cannot speak for him—that violence is going to be a key factor in how much progress our two nations can make.

I also hope that the intensity of violence in the Valley can be lessened to permit the prospect of peace to truly break out in South Asia. I believe the All Party Hurriyat Conference also has a role to play. I am sorry it has divided recently. I hope they unite again, but I welcome the fact that New Delhi has extended the invitation to APHC to come and talk to them unconditionally.

Q: The State of Jammu and Kashmir involves at least five clear-cut units. The northern areas which our ancestors conquered from Central Asia; Ladakh which is an extension of Tibetan culture; the Jammu region; Muzaffarabad; Mirpur; and the Kashmir Valley. There is a strong body of opinion in this country also that feels that we should get over this problem. The wheel of history is turning. If we do not take advantage of the present situation our children and grandchildren will live permanently under the threat of nuclear annihilation. You may recall the idea of subcontinental confederation that Dr Karan Singh put forward ten years ago in an article for the *Hindustan Times*. And I would say that we have to grasp this opportunity within the next few months. I hope that Mr Vajpayee and the political leadership in our country, and General Musharraf and the political leadership in Pakistan will

realise that tremendous benefits as you have said, would flow from a final resolution—from what the Simla Agreement calls a final settlement of Jammu and Kashmir.

Benazir Bhutto: I would agree that Simla was a very important step in 1972. But now, time is calling for us to move beyond Simla to a new era, and that it is very important to overcome threats from each other to move in that direction.

Omar Abdullah: In an interview which the current chief minister of Jammu and Kashmir gave to BBC, he endorsed quite spectacularly your view that the way ahead in Kashmir was shared sovereignty. Now this is a concept which one hears, but details of it are very slim. Since this was a concept that was originally I believe put forward by you, I would be very keen to know exactly how this shared sovereignty would come into play. The second part is that we have talked a lot about converting the Line of Control into an international border. Convert it into a soft border, and take a solution from there. This is a solution I believe will sell easier in India than it will in Pakistan. Could you give us an indication of what the bare minimum that would actually sell on ground in Pakistan is, so once and for all we can end this bloody mess?

Benazir Bhutto: For example, in Europe people are together in a community of nations but they don't call it a confederation, and they don't call it shared sovereignty. But they *are* a community of independent nations with independent sovereignty who have decided to work together on trade and other important issues that effect world community. They have also managed to elect a parliament of their own. Perhaps this is what we aspire to in another fifty years or 100 years, I cannot say, because it took Europe fifty years to reach this stage. It took France and Germany fifty years to cross those barriers.

I do believe that the European Union gives us a model that countries in South Asia ought to emulate, and we need to look closely at how Europe began its journey towards greater trading and a common market.

So in effect we are calling for safe and open borders. Safe and open borders that allow people to travel from all the South Asian countries to trade together, which allow us to take fiscal and other measures, and that can also enable the rest of the world also to trade with us in an easier fashion.

I am looking at two soft borders. One is the Line of Control, and one is a soft border over the whole Indo-Pak gamut. Since India and Pakistan are divided on the solution of territory, we have suggested that this be looked at later. Let us instead look at how we can socially unite people of Jammu and Kashmir, how we culturally and economically unite the people of Srinagar and Muzaffarabad without going into the issue of whose territory it is. Of course, there is one part that is physically in control of one country, and another part that is physically in control of another country; asking one or the other to withdraw from it is going to be contentious. (Meanwhile) we need to see how we can lessen the violence, make the border safe, and encourage the people to go across.

Moving out of the Line of Control and giving the Valley its separate status that can allow the All Party Hurriyat Conference to function, is also an emotive word here. So I feel the need to avoid those issues where such strong emotions are involved and to follow those issues where we agree.

Jordan and Israel have open borders but there is no militancy, because Jordanian and Israeli forces have agreed on how to monitor it and how to make it safe. So, Indian and Pakistani forces can learn from Jordan and Israel! My plea is: let's end separation of Kashmiris, let us try and unite the Kashmiris. If everyone agrees, we will make progress. And even if people don't agree on it, I still believe that we should be making progress in other areas.

On the Kashmir issue, my own view is to support the All Party Hurriyat Conference. I see it as a matter for Kashmiris, how they want to live. Do the Kashmiris want to have a separate parliament on the Indian side, and a separate parliament on the Pakistani side, and share sovereignty through an upper parliament? I don't know. This is not an issue for me, this is an issue for Kashmiris. Are the Kashmiris happy with the Line of Control? What do the Kashmiris want? I am quite happy to go along with what the Kashmiris want.

I want to see that India and Pakistan should not go to war because a war could lead to the nuclear option. I want to see Pakistan and India play a role in the global war against terror by ensuring that the region is free from armed violence. And, I want to see India and Pakistan pave the way for a European Union type of model for South Asian cooperation and commerce.

Q: We talked yesterday about no borders and a single currency (for South Asia). Is it possible, and how soon? You and Rajiv Gandhi both had a lot of things in common—political background, families, youth, education, and last but not least, good looks. Where did you both go wrong in terms of solving the Kashmir problem?

Benazir Bhutto: I think we were making a lot of progress. The first agreement since 1982 was signed with Prime Minister Gandhi. He came from a political family and so did I. He had faced the murder of his mother and I had seen th murder of my father. There was a lot more. His brother had been killed and my brother Shahnawaz had been killed at that time. There was a lot we shared, and we moved forward.

We agreed not to attack each other's nuclear facilities. We established the hotlines between the military headquarters of both our countries. We opened our countries to greater trade. We set up committees that had worked enormously and set the framework for redeployment of troops from Siachen glacier areas—or Kargil, I don't remember the exact geographical area. And we had also started talks on mutual reduction of troops.

But then Rajiv Gandhi decided to call elections, which he lost, and somehow Prime Minister V.P. Singh was not able to establish the same kind of relations we had with Prime Minister Gandhi. And after that I lost office, and it has been a difficult journey since then, although I mention again that during my tenure in office the second time round, the intensity of rant was high, but the intensity of violence was not as high as it is now.

I think more progress can be made in the future. It is wrong to dwell on the past because that is gone. We are in a new century, a new world order, and we need to play a part in constructing our own relations in the light of these new realities.

On new borders and single currency, it all depends on what one means by borders and what one means by the currency. For instance, if I say here in New Delhi, yes I want no borders, it is going to go wrong in Pakistan. But tell me, when you have free travel, you have territorial borders and yet in many senses it's borderless. For example, if I want to go from London to France, London has its borders and France has its borders, but would we call that borders with free travel? Therefore it all depends on your own use of the phrase. What we would like to see is a situation as in the European Union, where I would like to see people from India and Pakistan visiting one another's country without visas.

That is why during the SAARC summit in December 1998 in Islamabad I proposed to Rajiv Gandhi that we should move towards a world where we could travel in all of South Asia without passports, and without visas. Some would call that a borderless world. Others would not. It was as a consequence of my proposal to Rajiv Gandhi that we allow judges and parliamentarians to travel without visas to each other's country. If you would like to call that a world without borders you may, but there are others who would say that territorial borders still exist, although the travel borders don't.

Q: I have two questions for you. First, during deliberations yesterday there were comments on a multilateral South Asian framework to assist the resolution of issues between various countries of South Asia. We have seen how this has worked in the case of a European model which you yourself have quoted but has not worked as successfully with regard to SAARC. I wanted to find out whether an effective multilateral South Asian framework can help us in this process. Secondly, are there areas of economic cooperation that you see between our two countries that can also lead to a greater sense of trust between us, apart from oil and gas?

 Benazir Bhutto: Yes, a multilateral South Asian framework can be helpful and workable in our region, and I think we need to devote time to it. On the economic South Asian block, there are many areas that we have listed in our trade. I think it included sugar, wheat, consumer items—I think there are a lot of consumer items that you produce more cheaply and there are others that we produce more cheaply. Across the gamut, from agriculture products to manufactured goods, there is tremendous potential for both our countries—indeed, for all the countries of South Asia.

Q: You have talked about army preference for the sort of low intensity conflict, using what you termed militants and what we call terrorists. Earlier, you have talked about Pakistan army's vested interest in keeping some kind of conflict going because it kept their budget going. You talked about retired generals who ran little private armies, you talked about ISI's overwhelming influence. Given this background, given what you have just said today about democracies not going to war with each other, how optimistic can we be about lasting peace as long as General Musharraf and the Pakistani army are in power?

Benazir Bhutto: I don't want to be a party pooper—there is all this great excitement and I want to contribute to that excitement. I want to create momentum for peace and I think by being welcoming, by being positive, by being optimistic I am creating a momentum for peace. At the same time, as I have pointed out, there was a greater diversion of view between the military establishment and political establishments—if I can call Pakistan Peoples Party a political establishment. In the time since I gave my interview (to Vir Sanghvi) in 2001, when very few Pakistani politicians would visit India, the military establishment has decided to adopt our political establishment's foreign policy. So they are saying things that we were saying before. They are saying, "We will ban the militant establishments, we think that cross-border militancy is wrong, and it is going to create trouble in our relations, we want greater economic confidence."

Of course, there are still disparities between the military establishment's and political establishment's viewpoints. For example, they have insisted that without progress on Kashmir there cannot be progress on trade, whereas we believe that war creates a climate of poverty and poverty creates a climate of war.

General Musharraf has made promises to the United States and the United Kingdom, which are playing very important fiscal and other roles in Pakistan. So, for me to say that I am less than optimistic would make me look like somebody who is putting her own private interests before the South Asian regime. I don't want to do that, but if I am not misinterpreted, I do believe that democracies don't go to war against other democracies. And I do feel that if Pakistan's present regime is unable to deliver what it said in its stated political foreign objective, then the people of Pakistan must think very strongly about bringing about a change in the government that can deliver more efficiently what both sides promise.

Q: You are a powerful leader, even though you are an exile at the moment, of a very strong political party in Pakistan. Yesterday, two specific proposals were made, one by the Prime Minister of India, and one by the Leader of the Opposition. The Prime Minister spoke of a South Asian single currency and open borders, and the Leader of the Opposition of a single parliament. What can you do to make your party in Pakistan adopt these two items as a political platform?

Benazir Bhutto: The way we are placed today is the way Europe was placed fifty years ago. For a European leader to have said, fifty years ago that we are going to have single parliament and we are going to have single currency would have jettisoned the idea of a common market. I don't want to jettison ideas and I don't want to hijack from future generations, decisions they may take.

I want to start on the concept of a European Union. I want to start by seeing countries of South Asia take similar steps politically, economically, socially and culturally as the Europeans did then. Will it result in single currency—who knows? Fifty years down the line, twenty-five years down the line it may. When you have common trading goals then you can have a common trading currency. Who knows, twenty-five years from now the people of South Asia may decide, that they want to have a common parliament. But for me to say that now would, I apprehend, create a situation that would not only block progress on item one, but would block progress even on item two.

So, I feel it is my responsibility to start the journey in Pakistan, and to start the journey I feel that I have to map out a foreseeable future and leave the progress of the second part of the journey to others who may come. If God gives me a chance to make those decisions when they arrive … But right now, what I would like to see is that we end the violence, that we cooperate, we should be able to travel freely in each others countries. Do I share your Prime Minister and Mrs Gandhi's vision? I can't say that now, but who knows what tomorrow will bring?

Leveraging **Peace** FOR PROFIT

Bimal Jalan
N.K. Singh
Anil D. Ambani
Manvinder Singh Banga

‘Regional integration, regional commerce, regional trade, openness of economy — either regionally or internationally — is not a zero-sum game. In the sense that your gain is my loss. Everybody gains.’

Bimal Jalan

Member of Parliament & Former Governor, Reserve Bank of India

There are three or four points I want to emphasise, underlining that peace is good for the economy.

The first point is that, it's not the quantitative factor, which would make a difference. It is not the reduction in defence expenditure by for example, Rs 1,000 crore, which makes a difference. It does make a difference to fiscal position, to the ability to invest in infrastructure. But, what makes a difference is somewhat more qualitative.

For want of a better word, let us call it the feel-good factor, like what happened in Europe after the war. Between 1950 and 1980, there are thirty years, which have been described by most economists, commentators and historians as thirty glorious years of European recovery, European welfare, and European development. This cannot be counted in terms of rates of investment or the rate of savings, or the amount of expenditure. There is a burst of energy because of that feel-good factor which is hardly controversial. If something like this happens with peace, then the entire region will gain, and gain tremendously, and much more than what can be counted in terms of rupees.

The second point, which is again not realised is that, regional integration, regional commerce, regional trade, openness of economy—either regionally or internationally—is not a zero-sum game; what economists called zero-sum game is in the sense that your gain is my loss. In the old days when you had bilateral trade agreements, you sat down and said I have reduced my tariffs here, I will re-increase my trade there, you do the same, and this is the amount of trade that will increase.

Experience shows—globally—that regional integration or regional trade has moved faster when you are in trade. Everybody gains; this is not 'your gain my loss'. And I will say this particularly for this region. Of course there has to be a certain adherence to what you might call good, basic tenets of macroeconomic policies and efficiencies. But, given the fact that the country will follow a reasonable macroeconomic policies, I have no doubt that reducing trade barriers and treating integration in a peaceful environment will be beneficial to all.

This is an important point because it doesn't depend on whether you are large or small. It does not depend on whether India is large and some other countries are small, or smaller still. It doesn't matter, as it has to do with the comparative advantage of nations. Obviously you can go wrong if your macroeconomic policies are wrong, if your efficiencies are wrong, your productivity is low, and if your fiscal deficits are high. But I am assuming that in the same set of good domestic policies integration can only be beneficial.

So, you need a sequencing of measures, there will be within a country some losers and some gainers. This is the problem with competition—there will be some losers, some gainers; more efficiency will gain, less efficiency will lose.

The first thing that we need to do in sequencing is to eliminate trade barriers within a time-bound frame.

The second thing we can do—where again the downside risks are very few—is to ensure free flow of investments—subject of course to one consideration. This is avoidance of monopolies. Competition will ensure that the product prices are reasonable, efficiencies are guaranteed and that you are a global competitor. For example, Bangladesh is a small country but it has more exports in garments than we do. So, the smallness doesn't matter. It is specialisation that matters more.

And then, free travel, subject to some security considerations, can be worked out. Sequencing is important.

The prime minister, in his speech mentioned unification of the exchange rate which is the same thing as a single currency.

We would require a lot of preparation. After all, in Europe the Euro came after fifty years of integration. Why this requires more effort and sequencing is because, once trade expands, investment expands, you will need to work on some integration of fiscal policies.

You can't say, my exchange rate is fixed, when one country has a large fiscal deficit, and another country a small fiscal deficit. So, monetary policy would have to perform. All these things can be achieved over a period of time. Ultimately of course, you would want to have integration of policies—including macroeconomic policies—which is just as you have in India on the whole.

So, you will need a certain amount of harmony of fiscal, monetary, banking, and financial policies, which cut across regional barriers. That may take some time, 10-15 years. Europe took 40-45 years, but with the change in the world environment, maybe we can do this in fewer years.

Let's start with trade, go on to investment, then to travel—or perhaps, the three together—and then we can think about an alignment of macroeconomic policies. On the whole, if there is durable peace, and we believe that there is, you would see an improvement, which is qualitative as well as quantitative. With the new opportunities that our region has, I have no doubt we will all benefit enormously.

"There is an absence of peace sensibility in South Asia. Mere quantitative factors do not affect these intangible attributes. The attributes of mind, the feeling of security, and the invisible ways in which this feeling of security begins to have tangible action in terms of economic growth and prosperity are the qualitative factors that matter."

N.K. Singh

Member, Planning Commission of India

What is South Asia losing if we do not have a peace roadmap?

In terms of per capita income, South Asia's per capita income happens to be an abysmal US$438 as compared to the average of developing countries i.e. US$1,250. South Asia gets 3 per cent of the total investment of developing countries, less than what is received by sub-Saharan Africa. The percentage of literacy in South Asia is 54 per cent, compared to 74 per cent of all developing countries. It is similar in terms of the index of human development, infant mortality, and quality of life. Trade as part of GDP in South Asia, during the 1980s went down by 4 per cent, in the 1990s rising only by 1.03%.

Clearly South Asia is way behind the mainstream of what developing countries in general are. If we ask ourselves why South Asia is in this particular state, perhaps one of the very important factors is the absence of peace sensibility in this region. Mere quantitative factors do not affect these intangible attributes. The attributes of mind, the feeling of security and the invisible ways in which this feeling of security begins to have tangible action in terms of economic growth and prosperity are the qualitative factors that matter.

In my view, peace from South Asia has five critical dividends.

The first dividend is the gains of trade. South Asia's potential of gaining from the advantage of not only creating within the region, but also the ability of this region to have much greater trade and access with the rest of the world, is something which has been significantly stymied. Take India and Pakistan. In terms of what is called the gravity analysis of economic geography, our trade potential is way below the potential, and the multiplier effect of the terms of trade, which most economists have analysed is one area where dividend is stymied.

The second is even more fundamental: the investment dividend. When investors look for opportunity in South Asia, clearly one important psychological factor is risk premium. Will they be safe? Is it proper for them to put in these large investment decisions, given this kind of configuration?

In the growing world of today, when we talk of Business Process Outsourcing, that is something, which is significantly stymied. When multinational companies, for instance, set up large BPO operations in India, they obviously want to hedge the risk of whether they are employing too many people in this country. When General Electric begins to employ 30,000 people in India, General Electric wants to hedge its bet by employing some people elsewhere. When American Express begins to make major investment decisions, it wants to hedge risks by being able to put investments, and employ people in other parts.

So, I think that the second important factor is the risk premium, and this kind of hedging of the risk premium stymies investment, stymies new possibilities with the gains of the new economy, particularly (what) the ice-age economy really is bringing forth to the world.

The third important characteristic is what I call the energy infrastructure characteristic. The energy potential of this region is vast. And the fact that we cannot access gas, when the large gas reserves of Iran, the large gas reserves of Central Asia, the gas reserves in Bangladesh are not being put across to India even though India is willing to give gas to Bangladesh needs to be addressed. These are important attributes, which prevent this region from having the use of energy as a tool for economic development in a significant way. Energy efficiency and co-efficients of energy optimisation is a third important area where I think a peace dividend has an important multiplier affect.

The fourth important area in my view is the dividend from the gains of infrastructure—the gains of optimising mother-port facilities; gains of optimising and using electricity by trading, for instance; the possibilities of much greater civil aviation, much better access in terms of physical and air connectivity and utilisation of the commonalities of infrastructure in this region in a much more significant way.

And finally there is what I call the consumption dividend. The fact, for instance that, even with this kind of modest growth, India has achieved about 6.02 per cent growth between 1995 and 2002. We have about 100 million people having crossed over from middle class to the consuming upper-middle class. With this kind of a growth rate, we are going to have about forty million more people cross into that kind of consumption bracket—which is therefore enlarging the market in an exponential way. Think of a situation where the synergies from the dividends which I have mentioned gives this region high-growth potential, it gives India the potential to grow, with the energy efficiency in utilisation, at over 8 per cent, and the region as a whole then becomes one of the world's biggest and largest growing markets. And that market has huge consumption multiplier benefits in terms of white goods, brown goods, a changing consumer pattern and the kind of multiplier benefits which come from that.

The fact is that there is a lot of wasteful expenditure in terms of development, in terms of what we are able to achieve in per capita income, in the use of this money for the development activity, for improvement of social infrastructure and for the development of real infrastructure. These are benefits, which we cannot overlook.

I regard these five dividends and their multipliers to be the kind of peace dividend, which I believe is really going to make a qualitative difference for this region. As John Lennon once said, "All I want to say is give peace a chance." I will end by saying, all I want to say is give the peace dividend a chance.

'The European Union began with World War II foes becoming allies in a common market. The market came first and gradually wore down other issues. South Asia is at the crossroads. Either we work towards peace; or we take the path of paranoia, insecurity and militarisation ... with a potential for reducing millions of people to specks of radio-active dust.'

Anil D. Ambani

Vice-chairman, Reliance Industries Limited

I am glad that in South Asia, we need only adjust to three manageable time zones. There is the Indian Standard Time; the second time zone is half an hour behind India; and the third, half an hour ahead of India. As we know well, being 'ahead', 'behind', or 'with' India is a matter of interpretation, and often, heartburn, in South Asia!

I cannot see through the prism of political leaders, diplomats, or intellectuals. I can only speak from the point of view of someone who works in a corporation that is engaged in employment generation, and value creation for customers and shareholders to the maximum possible limit. It is from this perspective that I speak.

South Asia is at this time engaged in a tragic waste of energy. South Asia is one of the most densely populated regions of the world. It houses roughly one-fifth of the world's population, and this share is likely to increase to one-fourth of the total world population by the year 2025.

Unfortunately, this region is emerging as one of the poorest, the least literate, and the most malnourished regions in the world. The per capita income in South Asia is lower than that of any other region, with only a 1.03 per cent share of the global income. The region has 40 per cent of the poorest people in the world. With an adult literacy rate of 48 per cent, nearly half of the world's illiterate population resides in South Asia. The region has the greatest number of malnourished children. Peace and cooperation alone can overcome these problems and start a new chapter of growth and prosperity in the region.

The benefits of peace in the region are immense and the cost of conflict is far too apparent to ignore. A region representing a fifth of humanity that is overwhelmingly poor and illiterate cannot afford needless distractions from its social and economic priorities. The real wealth of this region is its people. If sufficient investment is made in these people, they can radically change the development prospects of South Asia in the twenty-first century.

A regime of peace in South Asia will stimulate unprecedented improvement in the standard and quality of life of one fifth of humanity. South Asia has the potential to become the food grain basket of the world. It offers huge opportunity for remunerative investment in agriculture and agro-processing industries. South Asia even has the potential to become a major energy hub for this part of the world.

The priorities are obvious. Provide universal primary education, basic health care for all, safe drinking water for the entire population, adequate nutrition for malnourished children, family planning services for at least 80 per cent of married couples, and new credit institutions for the poor to create self-employment opportunities.

Such a package of measures is expected to cost an average of US$8.6 billion a year during the next fifteen years, or an additional 1.06 per cent combined GNP of South Asia, assuming that GNP grows by one per cent a year. While this is a significant cost, it is certainly not unrealistic.

The SAARC leaders can agree on a compact to reduce their defence spending in line with the rest of the world and earmark the resources thus released for urgent social priority needs. If military spending is cut, for instance, by 5 per cent per annum in real terms, it can generate a peace dividend of around US$8 billion a year, which can easily finance most of the basic social services.

Of course, as far as India is concerned one must not exaggerate the significance of the conventionally understood peace dividend in the fiscal sense. The financial changes to the exchequer from increased regional security could be minimal in the medium term for three reasons :

- India's defence budget is already quite modest, contrary to popular belief. At less than 3 per cent of GDP, there isn't much of a squeeze that can be exerted on it. While pensions and salaries will continue to be a major component of this expenditure, the desperate need for defence modernisation will mean that India will have to find resources for defence, even if peace with Pakistan is assured.
- India's security concerns transcend Pakistan, and in addressing these the country will have to spend even more on higher cost modern technology.
- Apart from the regular defence expenditure, India will have to continue to spend on internal security and on modernising the response to terrorism.

However, an environment of peace and cooperation can alter investor sentiment in the entire region. This would benefit not just India and Pakistan, but Bangladesh, Nepal and Sri Lanka.

South Asia has the potential to become an area of great prosperity, partly based on the idea of growing trade between SAARC's seven nations. The growth recovery in the region is still tenuous and can be wasted if the region's political leaders do not demonstrate the required courage to buy peace within each country and across.

The volume of trade between participating countries remains tiny. India's exports to the SAARC region in 2000-01 amounted to a paltry 4 per cent of its total external trade. The terms of the SAARC Preferential Trade arrangement has already listed thousands of products and commodities that are accorded various degrees of protection to safeguard the markets of India's neighbours. Various countries of South Asia have also linked bilateral trade treaties, mainly to bypass SAARC red tape. A more ambitious trade agreement on a common market for the whole of the region, due to be agreed to this year, now looks unlikely to come into force before 2007, if at all.

Regional trade volumes can even today grow much further, if necessary infrastructure of road, rail or inland water transportation, adequate transit facilities, proper land customs checkposts with telecommunications are set up, and banking, including foreign exchange facilities, are provided. Let the proposed Asian Highway come up as soon as possible.

In much the same way as roads and railways link regions, I am talking about regional energy grids, catering to the demands of the respective countries. In the energy business, there is an assumption that one unit or energy input can enhance economic value by up to seven times. If we pursue this over-arching energy network, I can assure you that India and South Asia will be transformed, and light will have entered areas that until now have only known darkness.

Trading in electricity in India is now possible, thanks to recently liberalised laws that encouraging movement of electricity from energy surplus areas to energy deficient one. In addition, there is already a precedence of Bhutan generating electricity and selling an abundant surplus, an intended surplus, I might add, to the Indian grid. I understand this has led to Bhutan achieving higher per capita income than that of India. A power project on the Indo-Nepal border supplies electricity to both Nepal and India.

Why can't this develop into a greater grid for the greater good of the region?

I believe that in some quarters, there is a fear of huge Indian trade surpluses being generated on the integration of South Asian markets. In integrated economies, part of this trade surplus can be recycled as investment. There is considerable scope to expand Indian investments in countries where there are enough raw materials, skilled labour and markets. Value-added products, as suggested in the case of Bangladesh gas, could be exported to other third country markets for mutual benefit. All this can add to the supply capacity and promote growth of all national economies, and over time contribute to more balanced trade.

This comprehensive capital can have tremendous cross-flows in the region. It is not a question of India dominating the region. It is all about India and other nations of South Asia plugging into each other's potential sources and energy. Regional growth acceleration has positive externalities for all, since investors at home and abroad will begin to take a more benign view of South Asia as a whole. But those who celebrate 5 per cent to 7 per cent growth in the region should know that the region as a whole would need peace for it to log 8 per cent to 10 per cent growth. That is the peace dividend waiting to be encashed.

With all respect, this is only small change. A lot more needs to be done. We need to think big, raise our sights, and go and deliver with a sense of courage and conviction.

Business has the courage to move ahead. But we need to ask ourselves: Do the leaders of South Asia have the conviction to walk the road of progress and prosperity, hand in hand with the businesses, and the people, of South Asia? Do they have the courage to de-politicise commercial and industrial decisions in the greater interest of the people of South Asia? They must.

South Asia is at the crossroads. Either we work towards peace; or we take the path of paranoia, insecurity and militarisation, and descend into an abyss with a gruesome potential for reducing millions of people to specks of radioactive dust. This could well become our fate, if we don't cooperate.

Almost half of the 1.03 billion population of South Asia is below twenty. With increasing literacy, healthcare and communications, South Asia's youth will demand a better future.

In the same way as Germany and France could join hands through economic necessity, after the fall of the Iron Curtain, investments and trade inputs from western Europe helped turn the ravaged economies of the former Soviet Bloc nations into vastly more stable ones.

The EU has grown so prodigiously that there is no place left to add more stars to the EU flag. EU leaders gave up long ago and decided they would stick to the twelve stars on the flag. In South Asia, we only need to deal with seven stars. Let us heed Edward Burke's advice: "Do not plan the future by the past." We cannot deny our children the seven-star future they so rightly deserve.

"The opening up of a free trade zone would strongly benefit the consumer in smaller countries. All these countries are significantly higher-cost economies. The moment they play in the bigger field, they would get scaled benefits, which would go straight to consumers: lower prices, higher demand, and a virtual cycle would emerge."

Manvinder Singh Banga

Chairman, Hindustan Lever; Unilever South Asia

Economic interdependence is a good way of breaking the deadlock arising out of political issues, especially between India and Pakistan, and from time to time, with our other neighbours as well.

Let us take heart from what we seem to have achieved on other fronts. With China, we also have a long-standing territorial dispute. But somehow, both of us have managed to park that issue and have got on with developing business. Today, trade between India and China is growing strongly. It is already US$4 or US$5 billion, and there is still great potential for the future.

My second point is that a free trade regime is a good way for all countries to enhance global competitiveness, especially vis-a-vis China.

Let us take a look at our region. It is an unusual region. India is very dominant; accounting for almost 80 per cent in terms of regional GDP; and there are six other states making up the balance, of which Pakistan is certainly a lead player. This is tailor-made for what I would call a David-Goliath syndrome. I think we need to recognise that. Whatever plan we develop, whatever actions we take, must begin from there.

Let us first look at it from the perspective of India. There is a great temptation within us to believe that there is marginal economic benefit from collaborating within South Asia. That actually, the greater economic gain would be to go beyond and find trading partners, bigger trading partners, whom we consider much more as our equals. Well, that's fine. I agree with that. We must proceed with as many bilateral agreements as we can.

But what we mustn't forget ever is that a precondition for our becoming an economic power in the world is: we have to have a peaceful neighbourhood. That is hugely critical.

If we have ambitions to be the information technology back-office of the world, or indeed, the manufacturing centre of the world—for automobile components, FMCG products, pharmaceuticals, to mention a few—all of this would be greatly beneficial if global buyers did not have to worry about the potential of instability in this region. Indeed, it would be greatly dampened if relations with our neighbours continue the way they are, and if from time to time, they worsened.

Let us look at this in another way. China's GDP is today 100 per cent greater than India's, giving it a huge-scale advantage. If India operates in a free SAARC region, at one stroke we make up 25 per cent of that gap. We narrow the gap of scale between ourselves and China by 25 per cent and that is not insubstantial in business terms. SAARC can therefore dramatically enhance its global competitiveness, and of course, for all its members.

Let us now shift gears a bit and look at this from the perspective of the smaller countries in the region. Their main worry is very straightforward. Their fear is that, if they open up their borders, they will be completely swamped by Indian goods. To them I say, and I say it again today, they will in any case be forced to open up their borders to the world. WTO, globalisation, liberalisation—it's happening. Therefore, for them it is absolutely crucial to gain global competitiveness for survival. What better way to do that than to do it by opening up their borders first within the region, as far as possible?

In all such countries, there are three stakeholders. And very often I find we actually do not talk about the most important stakeholder: the consumer. Actually, the consumer is hugely important, but he is seldom talked about. The opening up of a free trade zone would strongly benefit the consumer in these smaller countries through huge price reductions. All these countries are significantly higher-cost economies. The moment they play in the bigger field, they would get scaled benefits, which would go straight to consumers: lower prices, higher demand, and a virtual cycle would emerge.

Even for the government, there are huge benefits. There are benefits in terms of legalising trade—the cross-border trade that we talk about, or through third countries—and therefore, enhancing their customs revenues. But more than that perhaps, there is a huge benefit in their being able to save precious foreign exchange through import substitution. Most of the smaller countries import vast sums of their requirements from the rest of the world. Governments often tend to concentrate on the manufacturer, and the potential of a third stakeholder is blocked.

The government needs to listen much more to the consumer, and remember that it is the consumer who is the voter and not the manufacturer. As far as the manufacturer is concerned, there will be a little bit of pain, but there can be no gain without pain. We have stated it ourselves. Five years ago, you only had to walk in to any conference and you always heard industry talking about how we should keep barriers, tariffs—and issues such as these. Today, where has it gone? You walk in to any industry forum and you hear confidence, you hear the optimism of Indian companies going global. So, a change need not take long.

Let's take confidence from our own experience, let's share it with our neighbours and help them gain the same sense of confidence that today Indian industry feels. We can stand tall on a global stage. Let us ask them to join us as well.

Let me now give you a few examples, just to share with you how such a free trade zone could operate, quite importantly—and quickly—to mutual benefit.

I think the biggest opportunity comes from the homogeneity of the consumer mass, the consumer base. Across these countries, we have similar income levels, living standards, cultural issues, and tastes. Even languages are common. The Sri Lankan consumer behaves very similarly to the consumer in Tamil Nadu and Kerala. The consumer in Pakistan is very similar to the consumer in Punjab, or indeed, Sind-Pakistan is very similar to parts of Gujarat and Rajasthan. In Bangladesh, the consumer behaves exactly like the one in West Bengal. So homogeneity exists, and this is a big opportunity, perhaps a bigger opportunity in South Asia, than in any other trading bloc.

We have five Unilever companies operating in the region, working in very close cooperation. Already, we develop products for South Asia, we develop advertising for South Asia. We don't do it for just five countries or seven countries, and there is huge benefit of scale, huge synergy. A test result in Punjab is as valid for a test result in Pakistan. Or if we test something in Sri Lanka, it is as good for South India. Already we are realising huge synergies and cost reductions. This, in a world, that is so fettered and so restricted! Imagine what we could do if it was actually a free trade operation!

Let me take media, another source of great synergy, and something we don't often recognise, particularly because of the commonality of the satellite footprint. Hindi channels such as Star, Zee and Sony today have 60 per cent of the viewership of satellite homes in Pakistan. That's huge. What does that mean? Commercially, let me tell you what it means. If we spend a hundred rupees of advertising in India, effectively sixty rupees worth of advertising is going into Pakistan. Now if you had the same product, brand name, and advertising, you can imagine the benefits. In all these smaller countries you would be able to save your advertising budgets hugely, or indeed, get a much bigger bang for your rupee.

There is also a lot of benefit in the smaller countries through import substitution—and this is a very critical point not often articulated in this particular way. We know that cars, bicycles, tractors, and motorcycles in this country take half the cost to make as they do, say, in Pakistan. The Pakistani consumer can save hugely e.g. with pharmaceuticals. They currently make pharmaceuticals in Pakistan but they import all the bulk drugs. India has a booming bulk drug business and will have an even stronger one tomorrow. One study showed that if Pakistan were to import its tea from within the SAARC, instead of from China and Kenya, they could save something like US$100 million a year.

These are not small sums. These are big sums and here is the point. I think we spend too much time looking at bilateral trade balances between countries. The moment you begin to think, and instead, look through the lens of the global trade balance, we would all be much better off. How does it really matter if the trade balance between India and Pakistan worsens, as long as the global trade balance for Pakistan improves because of import substitution? That's the lens that we all need to talk about. Those are the figures that we need to share with our business partners and indeed, with governments.

We can also think in terms of using complementary capabilities. We know that India is very strong in long staple cotton, and Pakistan, in short staple cotton. India has very low cost capital equipment for textile machinery. Bangladesh and Sri Lanka have got the front end; they have got the lowest labour cost, highest productivity. In one stroke you can imagine if you were able to build an integrated supply chain, you could actually build a huge competitive advantage from cotton bush to shirts, and this is something that could surely help us compete with China, post the quota regime.

So going forward, how should we tackle this? What should we do? The advantages are obvious, and the commercial benefits are huge.

I think we have to enhance connectivity in the region. It took me forty-eight hours to go and come from Pakistan, for a 24-hour visit. We are not going to do a lot of business, even with Sri Lanka, if the only time you can travel on a direct flight from Mumbai is at 3 a.m. in the morning. And, it's a two-hour flight. It's not just about air and road travel. Do you know it takes me longer to airfreight products. It takes me almost eight or nine days to airfreight products to Bangladesh. It takes me two days to airfreight them to the US.

These are the real issues. I know there was a step-by-step programme outlined earlier, but I would actually argue that this should come right in front. Without connectivity, and really, enhanced connectivity—we can't even begin. We have just got to have connectivity. We must go step by step.

Also, I think we must look for a broad impact, not narrow impact. I know there has been a lot of talk about looking at categories and liberalising some. Indeed, I believe that, in the last five years, the number of products under SAPTA have gone up from 200 to about 3,500. Sounds impressive. Actually, those 3,500 account for 1 per cent of the trade. Quite honestly, that's not the way to go about it.

We must learn from Mercosur. What did they do? They said they were going to do it across the board. The moment you itemise in categories, you will be open to huge lobbying influences. There will always be a good reason why someone like me, or any other industrialist, will come and tell you: look, do it there first, not here. And I think we have got to stop that. We've got to take a brave position and say, we are going to do it across the board. I really believe that is the only way.

I think it is incumbent on India as the dominant player to lead the way. It is our responsibility. There is no doubt in my mind. We have much less to fear than anyone else. Here also, we must move away from the current thought process of multilateral negotiations and frameworks. We must move unilaterally.

We mustn't worry too much about reciprocity and constantly measuring what we are getting in return. We are big, we are confident, we are looking at the world. I have no doubt that reciprocity will come.

Frankly, I would look forward to the day—this may seem Utopian, but maybe it's not—when we could de-militarise the Indo-Pak border and replace it with a free trade zone with equal access for both Indian and the Pakistani business.

Q & A: Leveraging Peace for Profit

Q: Mr Ambani, in view of the peace dividend, as a business house, you will agree with me that you have very important stakes in peace, in cutting down defence expenditure in the country. Do you think that defence expenditure should be increased or lowered?

Anil Ambani: In my comments, I mentioned that for the region we are at the lowest figures in defence expenditure, as a percentage of GDP. I also spoke about reorienting and repositioning our defence expenditure because we have far greater challenges internally, which we need to tackle. We need to modernise our defence infrastructure and equipment. We have to really spend more money. So effectively, in aggregate terms, I don't think that we need to dramatically increase our defence expenditure.

And everything that I mentioned about savings, and comments that we made in terms of if we save this half percent, we can build twenty more hospitals, or 500 more schools, are clearly emotional and sentimental comments. I am sure they come up in standing committee meetings with the defence ministry, and elsewhere. But there is a reality-side to it also. If I just take Vindi's closing comments and say that, if there was a de-escalation on the borders we could replace the line of troops on both sides with free trading zones with equal access from both sides. So clearly, there is a possibility of saving large amounts of money on defence.

In absolute terms, I don't think that we are spending too much. We need to modernise our defence expenditure, and we need to arm our people. (Moreover) I think that, fewer people are joining the defence services and more people are taking early retirement, because they find other avenues for prosperity and growth. It's no longer a social security type situation for getting into defence services.

N.K. Singh: I think that clearly in terms of the percentage of the GDP, India's defence expenditure in comparison to other regions—other countries in this region—is rather modest. There is this whole issue of the acquisition that you face in terms of very creative financial engineering—to some extent masks the real quantum of the real defence expenditure. But I am sure that the need to re-design the nature of defence expenditure and the elements in terms of what we need to do with keeping pace with modern warfare, is a growing challenge for Indian defence forces—and that's something which we need to look into.

But, I think there is a more general point to be made. Since we are talking of the peace dividend, we cannot overlook the fact that in case peace does come to this region—and that, of course, is based upon many assumptions—then clearly it would be possible for this region to devote a much larger portion of its investible surpluses into developmental and social expenditure. This really does not require too much explanation.

Q: There are two things I would like to share on the various meetings of the Indo-Pak CEO's forum. Firstly, I think Pakistani business agrees with whatever has been said today by all the panelists. They do not fear the opening of the borders as businessmen. They don't feel that there will be an onslaught of Indian products—in fact, on the other hand there is a feeling that, they will have access to a huge market of one billion people.

Mr Banga talked about television. In fact, cable operators in Pakistan went on strike when they were asked not to broadcast Indian channels; that is the kind of consumer response that you are getting. On the Indian side you see Indian products being imported into Pakistan through third countries.

Secondly, the presentation that Pakistani businessmen made was that, the Pakistan economy is in good shape, and their corporate interest rates today are 2-3 per cent. Of course, the growth rate is not matching India's.

What emerged was their feeling that Prime Minister Vajpayee's initiative of this track two, is creating problems in Pakistan. They feel that if everybody focuses on track two, what will happen to Kashmir? We will lose the agenda of Kashmir. So, it was not really an economic consideration but a political one.

Mr Jalan, how do we keep the economic agenda alive while keeping the political considerations in parallel? I think the key issue is how to combine and find a solution together.

Bimal Jalan: I don't have much to say except that even the economic agenda can only be determined politically. After all, the governments have to get together; it is not just the corporate sector, nor the economists, and so on.

If politically the people of Pakistan don't want to move on this economic agenda, then it won't happen. But there is no conflict, as far as I can see, between that and the economic front. The decision has to be made politically.

Vindi Banga: To add to that, I also heard very similar voices when I travelled to Pakistan. My own view is that quite honestly—and I give this to you from my experience in business—whenever I am faced with a very difficult problem which looks intractable, or very challenging, it is very daunting to try and solve all of it at the same time. Therefore to me, what is absolutely crucial is for us to be able to try and solve the problem, bit by bit.

It is important for us to try and communicate to everyone through the CEO's forum and other forums, that it's all right if it's too big a problem for the moment—after all, if it wasn't, we would have solved it by now. It is not for want of trying. Some very eminent people I am sure have addressed it and tried their best to deal with it. Let's try and unravel the problem from the edges and perhaps we will then unravel the totality.

NK Singh: I agree with Bimal that, even the economic agenda will have to be determined by political considerations. I want to ask myself the hypothetical question: when will we reach a stage when economics will drive the politics of change? Because, I think that what you implied was if the comparative economic advantages are so obvious, there will be a stage—and stake—in which the economic compulsions begin to change the political agenda between the countries in this region.

Q: I would like to add a small comment and then pose a question, which any of the panelists could answer.

I think we are making a mistake in focussing the entire issue of peace dividend in South Asia to the Indo-Pakistan equation. Are we at war with Bangladesh, Nepal, Bhutan, or with Sri Lanka? Or for that matter, if we consider our extended neighbourhood, at war with Myanmar? We have very peaceful, friendly relations with all these countries and yet, we have not been able to develop a framework of economic cooperation with many of these countries.

For example, with Nepal we could do a lot in terms of cooperation in water resources, and that could transform in a major way the economy of Nepal, and could benefit us enormously by giving us access to energy. Similarly, in the case of Bangladesh, if Bangladesh does not give us transit access to the north-eastern part of (India) or they don't want to sell gas, it is not because there is an issue of war or peace or conflict—there are other issues involved. In the case of Sri Lanka of course, we have totally different things happening, where Sri Lanka actually wants to integrate its economy with India. And the present government of Sri Lanka has taken some very major steps in that direction, and we are negotiating a comprehensive economic partnership agreement with Sri Lanka. Bhutan of course has followed, I think, very wise policies, and they are cooperating with us. The results are apparent where the per capita income of Bhutan may go up to about US$1,200 once the latest hydroelectric project comes on stream.

Now, it is a fact that the conflict between India and Pakistan is colouring the perception in the outside world about investment in South Asia. But I think we should not ourselves get into a kind of mental framework where we feel that we cannot make progress in South Asia, unless our problem with Pakistan is resolved. True, this is a very important question. But this is not the sole issue on which we should focus.

We have certain alternative strategies, which we are devolving, and some success. We have, for example, BIMSTEC. We are going to hold a summit of BIMSTEC next year. We have made this very dramatic opening towards ASEAN and we will be negotiating a free trade agreement with ASEAN; the framework agreement is already being signed. And we have also this growth quadrangle concept,

involving Bangladesh, India and Nepal and Bhutan, which has certain future prospects.

So, do you agree or do you not agree that, we may be making a mistake in focussing the entire issue of the peace dividend in South Asia simply on the India Pakistan equation?

N.K .Singh: I will just make three brief comments on it. I think it is an important issue, and that it should not be a case where the process of economic cooperation in this region should be made hostage (to) the pace at which progress is made in securing a peace dividend between India and Pakistan. But I think that you will agree with one broad observation that I have to make on a point which Bimal had touched upon. What is important is not merely India and Pakistan, but the quality of trust between India and many other countries in this region.

If, for instance, India has not been able to utilise the tremendous hydroelectric potential which Nepal has for all these years, and to really harness the tremendous water resources to meet not only Nepal's bigger needs, it is because our relationship—although very cordial—has not had the kind of trust, which has enabled utilisation of the huge potential. If, for instance, India has not been able to persuade Bangladesh—it will be sensible for Bangladesh to meet its own energy requirement and then make gas available to India, or even, take gas from Tripura in view of which Bangladesh can make gas available to India—it is because I think trust has also been missing in that relationship.

So, I will really divide it into two categories. One, the agenda is beyond India-Pakistan. But with many countries we need to develop confidence and trust in much greater measure than has been available not merely recently. Second, there are areas we need to really highlight where we haven't made adequate effort—for instance, to utilise the great hydroelectric potential of Bhutan.

I agree that Sri Lanka is taking remarkable steps in not merely reforming its economy, but in developing areas of huge complementarity that exist between India and Sri Lanka; and being able to utilise its large growing market.

(However) to paint, therefore, the entire region with one paintbrush, would be perhaps be an over-simplification on our part. But certainly, trust and confidence would be one dominant element, which would bring multiple benefits.

Bimal Jalan: India's economic relationship with the rest of the world cannot be defined in these terms, and for that matter not even in terms of South Asia. We have to move with East Asia, Latin America.We have to be effective in the WTO. The point that I was making was that, the killer effect of all this—if that happens, I don't know whether it will happen—will be multiples of whatever you can achieve bilaterally from all these countries.

One more point about India. I think we also have to change our mindset. The kind of new thinking (we) have brought in our cooperation with East Asia, cooperation with the rest of the world, has enhanced India's stature, prestige, and economic prosperity.

I can say with a certain amount of definitiveness that, today India does not have a problem of money, per se. And therefore, we should think big, we should have a new vision, we should discard the old mindset—and I would go further. We should be the ones to take the initiative. We have no foreign exchange problem—you will not have one, even if you tried in the next five or ten years. We don't have a money liquidity problem; you won't have one, even if you try in the next five or ten years. Your interest rates today compare with the United States for ten-year bonds. So, we are in a position, where there are no economic barriers.

Defence expenditure is not the issue. The issue is that 55 per cent to 60 per cent of government expenditure does not result in anything and that is nothing to do with defence—it is as unproductive in roads, as it is in something else. So, it is not sectoral dispersal that you have to decide on, whatever your priorities are. The problem is that 60 per cent of our expenditure is dead, what economists call 'dead weight' loss; it just sinks. It is not transfer payments, wages, and profits; it is not value added; it just goes somewhere, which you and I know.

Anil Ambani: I agree with your comments. And just to take a pointer from what Mr N.K. Singh said is that, we have all known for many years—I should say, decades—about the potential of energy cooperation between, say, Nepal and India.

And as I look back at that opportunity—and we have tried to explore that for the last decades ourselves (Reliance)—I (would like to) answer your question with another question: What is really stopping us from achieving progress? Is it economics or is it politics?

I can assure you on behalf of the business community, from an economic standpoint we are ready to seize every opportunity that comes our way.

Vindi Banga: (If) we have seven people in the room, you are going to find it more difficult to agree. (If) you have two people in the room you should be able to find it easier to make an agreement. So, we must press ahead with as much bilateral movement, going forward, as we can between India-Pakistan, India-Bangladesh, India-Sri Lanka, India-Nepal, whatever we can do. Let's take heart from what is happening in the world. This is precisely what Singapore and Thailand are doing. As everybody knows, they have now said that we are going to go in for the 2+x formula, because they also found that in ASEAN it was very difficult to carry everybody together. So they said, all right, let's deal with this. If two of us agree, every one else can join the party, and they can join it at whatever pace they want.

I think it is great idea and we should practise more of it. We should have the confidence. Bimal (Jalan) said we have plenty of money, so why don't we develop unilateral moves with our bilateral partners? Take Bangladesh. They want oil. I was there recently and at a dinner they said, "Look, why doesn't India actually sell us some oil so that we can conserve precious dollars? On our part, maybe we can invite Indian investment into power plants and you can re-export electricity." This is the kind of creative bilateral thinking that we need.

Q: More than a question, this is a comment—and I want to refer to what one of the panelists talked about: the lack of confidence and trust. And I would like to second Anil's comment; I really think that, fairly and squarely the problem lies with politicians. It does not lie with the business sector, it does not lie with the population of these countries, but it lies with the politicians. The quicker we face it the better it is, in terms of moving forward.

(In terms of hydroelectricity) if we look at Nepal and Bhutan, their internal requirement is of only, say, 100 mw per country and their capability is to provide 100,000 mw. We need 100,000 mw. Why can't we allow them to supply it into our grid? Vindi talked about the point of incremental change. I think we have been dong incremental change in this country for too long. We need monumental change.

Maybe I am speaking with a little too much passion, but I represent a lot of youth of this country and we want to move forward, and we want to move forward quickly. We need people with vision and leadership. We need the private sector because the government cannot do it alone. So I would very strongly urge both of you (Anil Ambani and Vindi Banga) to drive the agenda because we need that in India.

Q: I am making an observation on the discussion about defence expenditure. I totally agree with what Anil (Ambani) said that, at the moment there is no need for us to increase or decrease the defence expenditure. What you want to bring in is greater efficiency, to get a bigger bang for the buck. Secondly, I agree with everybody here that economics and development both will reduce your security needs, not only yours, but everybody else's. So for a change let us take the economic agenda forward.

Q: I am from Intel and I like Vindi's suggestion. We run one South Asia sales and marketing team, and we can run it very effectively. The political metaphor has been EU. My question, especially to the businessmen, picking on what N.K.Singh said is: when can we start the economic agenda determining the political agenda? Should we take a page from Taiwan and South China, where the business agenda and business integration happened before the political integration?

N.K. Singh: Sometimes, it seems like a mutually assured deadlock. The positions we have taken on either side seem very difficult to move from. When you reach this situation, I believe that trying to find the economic way forward will eventually help to get to that solution. Of course, as Bimal very rightly pointed out, economics cannot work on its own. But each of us can play our role. Business can make people aware of the advantages, to make them aware of the opportunities, so that they can be persuaded. (Also) as I said, if governments begin to shift their focus from listening merely to the constituency that has the largest voice, which is the manufacturer, and instead, think of the consumers, I think they will make the transition very easily.

Anil Ambani: I firmly believe that, we need to see a growing divorce between economics and politics, and to a very large extent we have been able to achieve that in India, in terms of the rapid progress that we have made from an industry standpoint. How we take that across the border, or across borders around us, is the question. I think political leaders really carry the torch of trying to unravel this gridlock between economics and politics.

Because I firmly believe—and I am saying this at the cost of repetition—that Indian industry's progress in conquering the world, and India really becoming an economic superpower is being held up by the politics of nations, and politics of individuals.

Bimal Jalan: If the two countries could agree that there is an issue, we just put it in cold storage for X number of years, say, twenty years—I think that's where the answer lies. And I mean it seriously; you cannot resolve this issue with the present generation and therefore, leave it to a future generation. Until then, let us just move on.

Vindi Banga: I do not think it is sensible anymore to really say that what is good politics is not necessarily good economics, and what is good economics is not necessarily sensible politics. We are fast reaching a stage when what is sensible economics is also sensible politics. This synergy between sensible economics and sensible politics will really enable the youth to drive the agenda change forward.

Q: Mr Banga, you talked about a regional brand and cooperation and sharing the prowess of regions. Both the EU and the Far East as regional identities were built on the backbone of a free exchange of people—almost on the back of tourism. Why can't we, as a beginning—which will have less political interference except for some mandarins at the MEA (India's Ministry of External Affairs)—actually build a regional brand, that encourages tourism? If people

are exposed to your country, they invest in your country. Currently, there is lack of exposure, unless you are a part of a visiting delegation. So, what about a regional tourism brand for the SAARC region?

Vindi Banga: I totally agree with you. In fact, that's the reason why in my list of 'hows', one of the first steps that I pointed out, was the need for us to dramatically enhance our connectivity. And connectivity by air, road, people exchange, is actually all about individuals building bridges, individuals coming for tourism. Definitely, a possible South Asian tourism brand would have scale benefits compared with just offering India on a platter, because you can then add in the attractions of Sri Lanka or the attractions of the Royal Bengal tigers in Bangladesh, and so on. In fact, the moment you begin things like this, you begin to dream. For example, all (South Asian countries) have airlines, and look at their losses. Are they commercially viable? Can't you have one South Asian airline and so on? Now this may be a step too far, but to go back to where we started, connectivity in many ways is the key. That's the first step. Let's just do it.

Concluding Address

Madeleine K. Albright

'I was called arrogant for presuming to know more about what is in the best interests of India and Pakistan than their own leaders. I was also accused of hypocrisy, because I represented the government with the world's largest nuclear arsenal ... But I also believe that American leadership on nuclear issues has been going in the wrong direction.'

Madeleine K. Albright

Former Secretary of State,
United States of America

As many of you know, I have been deeply interested in the subcontinent since I was eleven years old.

When my father was here with the original UN commission, he used to write wonderful letters telling us all about the warm people he was meeting, the colourful streets, the beautiful rivers, and the majestic mountains of this region, not to mention the noisy monkeys that occasionally found their way into his hotel.

My father's enthusiasm was contagious and, in high school, my brother and sister and I all wrote essays about India and her neighbours.

For a time, we went around our house bowing to each other in imitation of the historical figure we admired most, Mahatma Gandhi.

When I was in high school, my father wrote a book entitled *Danger in Kashmir*, describing the tragedy of that state and the risks posed to the world by its ongoing strife. As a graduate student, I did research for the book's second edition.

My family history gave me a special fascination with South Asia, and I was eager to engage in the region when I became Secretary of State.

In 1997, I came here to meet with Prime Ministers Gujral and Sharif, and made sure to meet the Indian Opposition leader, Atal Bihari Vajpayee as well.

While in Pakistan, I travelled to a refugee camp for Afghan girls near Peshawar, not far from the Khyber pass.

In a prior era, when American officials visited that area, they denounced Soviet communists. I denounced the Taliban, saying that their record on human rights was poor and their policies toward women and girls despicable.

I was conscious as I did so, however, of a grave American failure. That failure was the decision in the early 1990s to pull back from Afghanistan following Soviet withdrawal. We left behind a country awash in arms but lacking economic opportunity and any kind of political organisation or unity.

The vacuum was soon filled by the Afghan civil war, an upsurge in radicalism, the sheltering of terrorists, and the undermining of Pakistan's democracy.

This is one mistake I do not expect to see repeated. The United States is unlikely ever again to lose sight of South Asia's importance.

This is partly due to the 9/11 terror attacks. But there are more positive grounds as well. President Clinton's memorable five-day visit here in the spring of 2000 and Prime Minister Vajpayee's return visit that fall opened a new and welcome chapter in relations between India and the United States.

To its credit, the Bush administration has worked to broaden that opening and increase areas of cooperation between our two countries. As Prime Minister Vajpayee has said, "we are natural allies."

We have the chance now to give that alliance substance through the business we do, the scientific projects we undertake, the cultural exchanges we conduct and the far-reaching relationships we establish.

At the same time, the United States is also giving priority to events in Afghanistan and along that country's border with Pakistan where a daily battle is waged between the rule of law and the forces of extremism.

I have to wonder however, whether that priority is high enough.

Two years ago, the Taliban were driven from power and hopes were high that a truly new era would begin. Unfortunately, Afghanistan's new era has much in common with the old. Osama bin Laden and Mullah Omar are still at large. Warlords control vast chunks of the nation. Heroin poppy production has risen in the last two years by 3,600 per cent. Crime is widespread. Humanitarian organisations are being harassed. The government is almost entirely dependent on outside help. And there is still no effective international peacekeeping beyond Kabul.

The sad truth is that in Afghanistan, the world community has been trying to get by on the cheap. After the Bosnia war, external support for reconstruction during the first two years equalled almost US$1,400 per person. In Afghanistan, that figure is US$64. In Kosovo, we had twenty international peacekeepers per 1,000 people. In Afghanistan, we have less than one. The Afghan Army was supposed to have 70,000 troops by now. It has 4,000.

So, instead of a nation-building process that is comprehensive and irreversible, we have one that is narrow and vulnerable. And, according to reports, Al Qaeda has not just survived in the region, it is planning new attacks all over the world.

The time is right for a new and high-level Bonn Conference—with Afghanistan's neighbours, India and other interested countries represented—for the purpose of helping Afghanistan succeed. And success does not mean simply writing a constitution. It means making that constitution real in the lives of the Afghan people. It means providing reliable security, legitimate economic opportunities, and basic government services such as education and health care. It means giving Afghan women a meaningful voice in helping to run their nation. It means taking heavy weapons out of the hands of warlords. And it means ensuring that Al-Qaeda and their Taliban protectors are driven out of business not just temporarily but permanently. This matters because Afghanistan matters, but also because we have learned that instability there can wreak havoc as far away as Manhattan and as close at hand as the Line of Control.

This leads me to the central theme of this conference. The costs of war and the potential benefits of peace. The basic points of these issues are so vital they cannot be stressed too often.

The cost of war—whether we call it war or merely the absence of peace—is measured first in the tens of thousands of lives lost due to violence and terror. For each life lost, there are many others damaged by wounds to body and mind. The human toll alone should erase any thought of a military solution. But, the cost of war is also measured in the millions of people deprived by schools not built, medicines not purchased, housing not assembled, and environmental projects never begun, because the money was being used to finance the arts of war, instead of the habits of peace. The cost of war is measured in the lack of trade and cooperative economic and energy projects among countries in the region. It is measured in the uncertainty that prevents South Asia from meeting its vast potential to attract investment, spur growth and lift standards of living. It is measured in South Asia's inability to act as a coherent bloc in world affairs and in the obstacle this creates to India assuming its proper place as a global leader. More deeply, the cost of war is found in the perversion of the conscience by fear and hate, the loss of hope, the growth of despair, and the corroding sense that violence is somehow the remedy to powerlessness. And in this region, the cost of war is felt, as well, in the possibility of nuclear catastrophe.

Five years ago, I said the South Asian nuclear tests were a mistake that would leave both India and Pakistan less secure, while undermining the global nuclear nonproliferation regime. Not everyone in this region appreciated those remarks.

I was called arrogant for presuming to know more about what is in the best interests of India and Pakistan than their own leaders. I was also accused of hypocrisy, because I represented the government with the world's largest nuclear arsenal. Hypocrite or not, that is what I believed then; it is what I believe now.

But I also believe that American leadership on nuclear issues has been going in the wrong direction. Despite vigorous lobbying by President Clinton, the US Senate failed to ratify the Nuclear Test Ban Treaty.

The current administration actually opposes that agreement. The White House has also withdrawn from the anti-Ballistic Missile Treaty and is actively considering the construction of a new generation of so-called 'bunker-busting' nuclear arms. So the question today is not that of one party lecturing another; it is simply a matter of dealing with reality. And reality will require cool heads and pragmatic policies with respect to military questions and controversial political dilemmas, as well.

My father once observed that, when it comes to Kashmir, "time has proven to be no healer." When he studied this dispute, he was still in the early stages of his career. Now, he is dead and I am old and Kashmir is still among the most dangerous and tragic places on earth.

India argues that the legal status of Kashmir and Jammu has long since been settled. But that assertion has not settled the controversy or ended the violence. It is worth remembering that the costs of war are not borne equally. The people of Kashmir have suffered uniquely, buffeted on one side by terrorists, on another by security forces that sometimes fail to observe basic standards of human rights.

Chief Minister Mohammad Sayeed has promised a healing touch. And he deserves the full support of India, Pakistan and the outside world in trying to make that work. Omar Abdullah speaks of the new generation of Kashmiris who need to be heard. I was also encouraged by Ms Bhutto's statements. The Kashmiris must be satisfied with their leadership—and feel less fear and frustration—because that is the main key to lasting stability.

When President Clinton visited Pakistan in 2000, he said, "this era does not reward people who struggle in vain to redraw borders with blood. It belongs to those with the vision to look beyond borders, for partners and commerce and trade."

In both India and Pakistan, President Clinton emphasised the four 'r's – restraint, respect for the line of control, renunciation of violence and renewal of dialogue. This remains, it seems to me, a pretty good recipe for moving in the right direction. And I am pleased to observe that, in recent weeks, this region has indeed been moving in the right direction.

The recent elections are an important demonstration of popular yearning among Kashmiris for a peaceful settlement and an end to violence. The ceasefire along the Line of Control agreed to last month is a very hopeful sign. So is the decision to restore commercial air and other transportation links. So is the plan to initiate regular contacts between maritime security agencies. And so is India's willingness to sit down with the leaders of Kashmiri separatist groups.

The process Prime Minister Vajpayee set in motion when he offered to extend 'a hand of friendship' to Pakistan is as welcome as it is vital. And Prime Minister Jamali's constructive response has provided a major boost. Both leaders seem determined to reduce tensions and open the door to real progress.

But many more steps will be required before the peoples of this region can hope to reap the dividends of true security and stability. The ceasefire must be institutionalised. Cross-border infiltration and terrorism must cease. Confidence-building measures on military concepts and nuclear doctrines must be implemented. Risk reduction centers must be established. And the name 'Kashmir' must again come to signify simply the name of a breathtaking place, not a heartbreaking crisis. One by one, the elements of a normal and neighbourly relationship must be assembled.

The question, however, is not so much whether Indian and Pakistani leaders have the right intentions. The question is whether they will prove strong and determined enough to survive the political battering that peacemakers inevitably receive. One of the sad lessons of history is that often those who care most are driven by the most destructive motives.

The urge for revenge is powerful. The desire to redress past wrongs can prove irresistible even while it results in new wrongs that others then seek to redress. This is how cycles of violence are started, and how extremists on one side nourish extremists on the other. Murder justifies murder and, as Gandhi pointed out, multiplies evil. Caught in the middle are those who may also be passionate about principle, but who are wise enough to know that killing brings dishonour to any cause, and that acts of vengeance accomplish nothing except the shedding of more blood.

Moderates want to enhance the quality of life. Extremists need violence to give their lives meaning. Moderates are armed with words and reason; extremists with rifles and bombs. It is not a fair fight. All too often, extremists control the agenda, as efforts toward peace are derailed by terrorists doing what terrorists do. That is why life-taking, wealth-draining, hope-killing conflicts drag on so long not only in South Asia, but also in the Middle East and Northern Ireland, the Caucasus and

Central Africa. Moderates, wary of being portrayed as apologists for the other side, frequently fail in their resolve, retreat when challenged, and never decide that now is the right time to take a stand. That is why the world needs nothing so much as fanatical moderates, leaders who will bring to the cause of reconciliation the same passion, energy, and willingness to run risks as those devoted to destruction. And, do not doubt, the risks are real. The list of immoderately moderate martyrs is a hallowed one.

On the desk of Prime Minister Nehru were two figures, a gold statuette of Mahatma Gandhi, and a bronze cast of the hand of Abraham Lincoln.

We think also of others, including Egypt's Anwar Sadat, Israel's Yitzhak Rabin, El Salvador's Archbishop Romero, Burma's General Aung San, America's Dr Martin Luther King Jr, and the many heroes who have tried over the years to bring peace to Kashmir only to be brutalised by their brethren.

During the Camp David Peace Talks, Yasser Arafat told me that the reason he could not agree to what Israel had offered is that he would be assassinated. On a personal level, I can certainly understand and sympathise with these fears. But succumbing to such tremors makes one a prisoner of history when the duty of a leader is to shape history.

Avoid risk and you cede the advantage to fear over hope, hate over tolerance, and might over right. Avoid risk and you give the radical few a license to limit opportunities for everyone. And the more times that happens the more it comes to be accepted as simply the way things are and the way things will always be.

It is not as if there were no constituency for peace. People throughout South Asia want to live normal lives free from terror and the fear of violence. The problem is that leaders often react to loudness and intensity of opinion, not simply breadth. Also, many citizens are cautious in backing peace; they need a champion to show the way.

Forty years ago, at the height of the Cold War, American President John Kennedy addressed these same issues in a different setting. "I speak of peace", he said. "Not a Pax Americana enforced on the world by American weapons of war [but a] genuine peace, the kind that enables men and nations to grow and hope and build a better life for their children."

He spoke of peace, because of the new face of war. War makes no sense in an age when great powers can maintain large and invulnerable nuclear forces. It makes no sense in an age when a single weapon contains ten times the explosive power delivered by all the forces in World War II. It makes no sense in an age when the deadly poisons unleashed by a nuclear exchange would be carried by wind and water and soil and seed to the far corners of the globe.

"I speak of peace, therefore", continued Kennedy, "as the necessary rational end of rational men."

In his remarks, Kennedy identified a host of obstacles to that rational end, among them the defeatist view that a pragmatic peace between two such great foes as the United States and Soviet Union was simply not possible.

"History teaches us", said Kennedy, "that enmities between nations, as between individuals, do not last forever."

He then urged Americans to do something very peculiar: to reexamine our attitudes toward the enemy; to acknowledge the many accomplishments of the Russian people; and to recognise that for all the differences, we shared a profound abhorrence of war and a deep interest in ending the arms race.

President Kennedy asked Americans to reconsider our whole conception of the Cold War and to understand that diplomacy should not be some sort of game in which each side competed to pile up the most points. It should not be about vilifying the other or pushing opponents into a corner where the only choices are war or humiliating retreat. He called for an approach that, without relaxing vigilance, would relax tensions. And he began by proposing a treaty to outlaw nuclear tests.

Kennedy's message forty years ago is the same as the message of this conference today. The costs of war are unaffordable; the dividends of peace are invaluable. But to secure those dividends, decent people on both sides must show the same devotion to building bridges as others do to blowing up bridges and stoking mistrust. Leaders must stop explaining why obstacles have made a solution impossible, and insist that it is no longer possible to allow any obstacle to prevent a solution. Governments must cease competing for advantage over the other and strive instead to surpass the other on the road to reconciliation. Negotiators must reevaluate fixed positions, understand that agreements do not come without compromise, and consider with honesty how the same issues would look from the opposite side of the table.

Freedom for India and Pakistan arrived that fateful midnight fifty-six years ago. It came as the result of a common struggle waged by Hindus, Muslims, Sikhs and others who shared a common purpose: liberation from colonial rule.

Imagine what South Asia would be like today if the peoples of this region had continued to focus their energy and resources on shared goals. Imagine what South Asia would have accomplished if the disagreement over Jammu and Kashmir had been settled to the satisfaction of all during those early years. Imagine where South Asia would now stand if for the last five decades the border between India and Pakistan had been free of tensions, turmoil and barriers to trade. Imagine how dynamic South Asia can be in the future if India and Pakistan are able to achieve real peace. Imagine the consequences if they are not.

On the eve of India's independence, Prime Minister Nehru said that a moment comes but rarely in history "when we step out from the old to the new."

The question that echoes now—not only here but around the world—is whether we will be able to step out from the old to the new; whether we will be able to free ourselves from the shackles of the past and forge agreements to end conflicts, defeat terror and help long-troubled regions achieve the rational end of rational people.

In considering that prospect, it is worth recalling the words of Vaclav Havel, "I am not the optimist", he said, "because I am not sure that everything ends well. Nor am I a pessimist, because I am not sure everything ends badly. Instead, I am a realist who carries hope, and hope is the belief that freedom and justice have meaning ... and that liberty is always worth the trouble."

I, too, am a realist who carries hope. And this conference—set against the promising actions, words and gestures of recent weeks—is the incubator of more hope.

The thing about peace is that once you truly decide to pursue it, the obstacles that once seemed so immovable begin to shift; the road that once seemed impassable starts to clear. The road to peace in South Asia remains sharply uphill, but it is surely worth the climb, because the alternative is not a different future—it is no future at all.

Q & A: Madeleine Albright

Q: Madam Secretary I have two questions. There are two dimensions of the Kashmir problem, the external and the internal. Touching upon the external one first, it is no secret that there is a great degree of distrust in this region about the motivations of the United States government, successive governments, and that leads to its own problems. How would you suggest to either the current US administration, or a future US administration, what steps it could take to build trust about its motivations in this region? We believe that for most of the time, the US intervenes very strongly when its own interest is threatened. Then, the moment its interest is no longer threatened, it leaves us to sort out our own problems.

The second part is how do you balance the contradictions? Pakistan looks for active intervention of the international community in the resolution of the Kashmir problem. India firmly believes that it is a bilateral matter and we will not tolerate any overt foreign intervention in this problem. Is there a way in which you can balance both these concerns?

My second question is with regard to the internal situation, which you touched upon. The sentiment, particularly in the United States, and of the international community in general is that the solution must be in keeping with the wishes of the Kashmiri people. Now I am an elected representative of the Kashmiri people in parliament, I also lead a political party that has twenty-eight elected representatives in the Assembly, but I cannot claim to represent the wishes of the Kashmiri people. In the absence of the chief minister I would take the liberty of suggesting, in all fairness, and he would agree with me that Pakistani leadership both in office and outside office, is under the highly mistaken impression that

the All Party Hurriyat Conference represents the Kashmiri people. How then would you suggest that we are certain the wishes of Kashmiri people on both sides of the Line of Control can move this process forward?

Madeleine Albright: I think that probably in America we define our national interest as *we* see it. This is differently than when *you* see our national interest. And I think that the hardest part is trying to get some mutual recognition of what our national interests are. I believe that in America's national interest, peace and stability in a particular region is foremost because, we have learnt to our own tragedy, that when there is instability in any part of the world, it comes homes to America.

The truth is that as I often tell my friends and my students in every country, America basically is interested in its own national interest. That is why it says 'national interest'. The question is how it is defined, and how widely it takes in the national interest of other countries. So, I believe that America's motivation has obviously changed over the years in terms of when this whole region was seen primarily through the prism of the Cold War, and the fact that India was viewed more as having a closer tie with the Soviet Union, while Pakistan at various periods was seen closer to the United States.

However, I very well remember writing a paper in graduate school about the influence of China and Pakistan, so it never was quite as simple as a kind of divided relationship. I think at the end of the Cold War, there was very much a desire to see more of quality in terms of how the two countries were treated. And, as I said in my remarks, I think President Clinton tried very hard, and succeeded to a certain extent, in beginning to show the relevance of our relationship with India. I think that the Bush administration is also showing its interest in the region.

What I am concerned about is, Americans are the most generous people in the world with the shortest attention span. As I said in my remarks, we will not stay long enough in Afghanistan to make sure that a vacuum does not exist there, and if a vacuum returns or does exit, I think then it spreads generally where the region is.

I have been very encouraged by the comments that I have heard here about the interest in some kind of a common approach whether it resembles the European Union or some other aspect. Because I think that it is something the United States should encourage.

So to round that out, I think that we probably see a national and Christian way where we would like to see a lack of fighting between India and Pakistan, stability, and an attempt to make sure that there is democracy throughout the subcontinent.

I do think it is a very difficult problem, which I remember dealing with myself, in terms of the fact that Pakistan *does* want to have international involvement in Kashmir and India does not. It is very hard for the United States to play a role, if one of the parties does not want to involve it. But, that does not mean that we should not, in fact, be supportive of the various measures between the two countries to try to get together—as has been evidenced in the last few weeks. Steps have been taken forward.

To point out the advantages, whether it is in better political relations or better trade and economic relations, to support a peace process, which is what we have tried to do in other areas. And I think there are models, whereby the US in various administrations has been supportive of other peace processes in other places, whether it is Northern Ireland, or in the Middle East or in the Balkans. But it is very hard, despite the desire of some, to get involved. On getting a settlement in Kashmir, if India does not want us involved—believe me, because that was something that we attempted at various times—we can't do it.

I think you have asked the hardest question about how you do in fact determine the wishes of the Kashmiri people. I had always thought that plebiscite or a referendum of some kind would the most logical way. Whether there is another method, a kind of indirect way in terms of the elections to various bodies that would represent that—I think those are the kinds of things that you have to look for. But, there is no other way to find as a settlement, than getting people to vote on it, whether you call it a plebiscite or referendum—that is the normal way to try to find out. I know the difficulties with it, but there is not a lot of ways to find out what the people want. Otherwise they do take to the street and there's violence.

Q: What was America doing in Iraq?

Madeleine Albright: I am the wrong person to explain this. Let me say this. It is very hard, I think for any former official of any party to be abroad, and be critical of one's own government. It is an uncomfortable position, and if you have been secretary of state, maybe even more uncomfortable. But I had said many times, that I agreed with the 'why' of the Iraq war, having said similar things about Saddam Hussein as President Bush had, for many years. It was my job as UN ambassador, and then as secretary of state to make sure that the various Security Council resolutions that were adopted at the end of the Gulf War were carried out, so I said approximately the same things.

Saddam obviously had crossed an international border, trashed another country, tortured his people, and used poison gas against them. I never, however, understood 'why now'?

From my perspective, we had Saddam in a strategic box, the no-fly zones were being vigorously controlled and large portions of the country were in fact under surveillance, so to speak. (I actually did believe that there were weapons of mass destruction because in 1998, when the inspectors left, not all the weapons had been accounted for. So, logic would lead one to believe that they in fact, did still exist). I think this war was one of choice not of necessity.

My other problem was that I did not understand 'what next', that in the various nation-building operations, there was in fact some kind of a component for the international community. When being briefed about the 'what next' plans, I found that piece missing.

I did believe—and do believe—President Bush when he says, "we have to fight terrorism". I think that has certainly been the theme of the discussions here, everybody believes that is what we need to be doing. For me the major front on terrorism was Afghanistan, and that we have been diverted from that. I never did believe that there is a connection between Osama bin Laden, Saddam Hussein, and Al Qaeda, but I am now willing to believe that the chaotic situation in Iraq in effect is a magnet for various groups to hate us.

I am concerned about the fact that the United States is losing some of its reputation and political capital throughout this particular struggle. It is essential that for the international community to win the peace in Iraq, it is essential for the countries of the world to support what is happening, because it is now in all our national interests to make sure that it does not deteriorate further.

Q. The Bush administration first responds to the United Nations on the Iraq situation, and then the Security Council rebuffs it for the second resolution on Iraq. What in your opinion is the state of the United Nations? And what do you think of the prospects for India's permanent membership in the Security Council?

Madeleine Albright: As you know, I am a great supporter of the UN though, as you also know, I did not think it was a perfect institution. It was very important for reforms to take place, and the United State pushed a great deal for that. It was not easy given the fact that I was reminded everyday that we had not paid all our bills, leading the British to deliver a sentence that they had been waiting 200 years to say, "representation without taxation".

I think that it is always very difficult to make the UN work properly. But, I was very glad when the administration had gone to the UN in order to get a resolution—and then I would have done the tactics somewhat differently.

There is a real question whether it was necessary to go for the second resolution. I was very troubled—and still I am—by the kind of paralysis that was brought on the Security Council by the twin statements of President Bush and President Chirac. President Bush said that he was not interested in what came out of the Security Council. President Chirac said that we would veto anything that came out of the Security Council. Between the two of them, I think they made it a very difficult situation for the UN.

I believe that UN is essential for us, though it is going through a very bad period. The various statements of the Secretary General and the various challenges that the Secretary

 General has issued, need to be examined carefully and understood. And the US has to support the UN.

There are people in the US who don't like the United Nations no matter what, and I often say this in my speeches around the United States. There are some people who will never like the UN, because it is full of foreigners—which frankly can't be helped. The UN needs to be put into a vital position. I believe in multilateral organisation and I believe in the UN.

Security Council reform however, is very much like a Rubic's cube, very hard to get everything lined up, when we were trying to get Japan and Germany to be permanent members of the Security Council. (I) remember when our Italian colleague came to me with the following argument—and this is a true story—he said why Germany and Japan, and not Italy? We lost the war too.

Out of fifteen members of the Council, there are five at any given time from Europe, and that is a lot. When I used to go the European ambassador to ask for support for something, he said I am sorry I can't do it, because we don't yet have a common EU position. A few days later, I would go to him and say well, now can you help? And he said no, because we have a common European position. So, it seems to be if they have a common position, they can have one seat, but I can't visualise either the United Kingdom or France giving up veto in order to arrive at that.

India should be a permanent member of the Security Council. It is the world's largest democracy and needs to play that role.

Q: We wanted to stop war, but we could not agree on a definition of aggression and even the United Nations took about twenty-five years to define it. Don't you think that now we must be able to evolve a verbal formulation, which immediately helps us distinguish a freedom fighter from a terrorist? Today there is lot of confusion about these two concepts and until we evolve this kind of formulation, do you tentatively agree that if there is a democratic set-up in which everybody has rights of political, social, and economic equality, then any use of violence to obtain any political objective must amount to terrorism, and such terrorists can't be elevated to the pedestal of freedom fighter?

Madeleine Albright: Definitional issues in the international community are always the most difficult because you have people from over 192 countries, usually using people who are very good at words—otherwise, you don't end up being a diplomat—trying to figure out definitions. For me, the definition is very simple. If innocent lives are used, specifically targeted in order to make the point, then that person is a terrorist, not a freedom fighter. When innocent people are used as victims to prove a point, not accidentally, but specifically targeted, then that is the definition.

The question is how generally to avoid situations that create such pain and anguish among people that they feel they have to take to fighting to get what they want. Now that is the most idealistic kind of a statement, because it is very difficult to have that kind of economic situation or to deal with the variety of border disputes. But I would have hoped that by now we could have come up with the common definition of terrorist, and not get ourselves into what to me is a circular argument about the definition between the terrorist and a freedom fighter. It is one of the most pernicious discussions that we can have, and it does not allow us to move forward. There has to be a way to try to determine it.

It goes back to the question that Mr Abdullah asks, which is how do you determine what the wishes of people are, and you therefore have to provide some other channels where they don't feel that taking to the street and killing other people is the only way to express their views.

Q: I was wondering whether you would like share anything with us, about whether China can either help or hinder this entire issue of South Asia and its progress?

Madeleine Albright: China is definitely now playing one of the more interesting roles, not just in the region but globally, in terms of exerting its influence in a wider way. Not just through ideological control, which is what they were trying to do in the 1960s, and trying to buy their friends in various ways.

I am encouraged by some of the feelers that have gone out between India and China to try to resolve long-standing border disputes and to try to see each other in a different way. I happen to believe that it is very important for China to play a strong and positive regional role in partnership with India, not against India, and that the developing dialogue is one worth pursuing, and that having a strategic partnership of some kind for all of us with China is well worth it. Because, they are going to play a very large role, and in my view it is better to have them inside, than outside.

Q: You mentioned that one way of ascertaining the wishes of the people is perhaps plebiscite or referendum and you are not quite sure whether there are other ways. Would you apply the same criteria to ascertaining the wishes of the Kurds in Iraq, Kurds in Turkey, Kosovars and Serbs?

Madeleine Albright: I will give my views. I do believe in the electoral process and believe that it is acceptable and important also in Iraq. The question is at what stage, how quickly do you prepare for election? As I responded earlier, I think this war is one of choice not of necessity, and that the plans for post-war Iraq were not drawn out in a comprehensive way, in a way to find out the views of the Iraqi people.

I think it is always very difficult when people that have been in exile are designated as leaders without some kind of fusion with what has been going on inside the country. This was true—believe it or not—after World War II in Europe when governments in exile returned to their respective countries and had trouble relating to what was going on.

Democracy cannot be imposed from above; it is a contradiction in terms. It has to come bottom-up and it can begin to happen through elections at local levels and moving up in some kind of organized way. The problem that we are into now is one of how to turn over power rapidly enough to Iraqis and yet having an election process—it does not make any sense at all. There are questions about what the electoral rolls would look like and who would be the controlling powers, but in the end I think we have to move to elections in Iraq. And that is what the coalition authority should be working towards rather than designating people to run the place.

Q: Assume you had been secretary of state and Bill Clinton had been president when 9/11 happened. Would you then have invaded

Afghanistan, installed Hamid Karzai as Mayor of Kabul, left, and then invaded Iraq? Or would you have done things differently?

Madeleine Albright: Yes, no, yes, no. First of all I think initial reaction to 9/11, and the military action in Afghanistan was the right decision—I speak for myself. I then would have done things differently in Afghanistan. Basically, understanding the significance of NATO nations having activated Article 5, and using them more effectively right away.

I also would have tried to get a security network for the entire country so that President Karzai is not just Mayor of Kabul and tried to get more control over what was happening. Which then leads to the "no" on Iraq because I think that was a diversion from what we should be doing, to fight terrorism. Therefore, while we all thought Saddam Hussein was a threat, we did not see him as an imminent threat and therefore, not necessary to invade. I called for the regime-change myself, but we saw something coming internally, not by invasion. And there were a group of people in Washington who were bound and determined to do that at any given time.

I would now be working very hard to try to get some kind of stability in Iraq, which means getting more countries involved, letting out contracts to other than those countries that were involved. That helps, because I think this has to be an international activity. It now concerns all of us.

Glossary of Terms

Agra Declaration: An agreement which was supposed to be signed between Indian Prime Minister Atal Bihari Vajpayee and General Pervaz Musharraf, President of Pakistan in 2001. This Declaration contained several confidence-building measures (CBMs) for ushering in an era of peace, but the Agra Summit collapsed.

Andean Pact: Formed in 1969, the Andean Pact aims to promote regional economic integration among medium-sized Latin American countries. Members include Bolivia, Colombia, Ecuador, Peru and Venezuela.

APEC: Asia-Pacific Economic Cooperation is the premier forum for facilitating economic growth, cooperation, trade and investment in the Asia-Pacific region.

ASEAN: Association of South-east Asian Nations.

ASEAN plus-three format: Annual summit of ASEAN leaders with their counterpats from China, Japan and the Republic of Korea.

ASEAN plus-one format: Annual summit meetings held between ASEAN leaders and China.

COMESA: Common Market for Eastern and Southern Africa.

FMCG: Fast moving consumer goods.

GOSL: Government of Sri Lanka.

Hizb-ul-Mujaheddin: The largest militant group in Indian Kashmir.

Hurriyat Conference: An alliance of 26 political, social and religious organisations. The Hurriyat Conference was formed on 9 March 1993 as a political front to further the cause of Kashmiri separatism.

IT: Information technology.

Khan Abdul Ghaffar Khan: Also known as the Frontier Gandhi, Khan organised a powerful movement of the Khudai Khidmatgars or True Servants of God, which was pledged to complete non-violence and whose members became some of the bravest and most daring and reliable non-violent resisters during India's struggle for independence.

Lahore Declaration: Indian Prime Minister Atal Bihari Vajpayee and Pakistani Prime Minister Nawaz Sharif met in Lahore and signed the joint declaration on 21 February 1999. The Declaration sought to resolve to settle all contentious issues, including Kashmir, between the two countries through bilateral dialogue and take immediate steps to reduce the risk of accidental or unauthorised use of nuclear weapons.

Line of Control: A 450-mile line that is supposed to indicate the boundary between the part of Kashmir controlled by India and the part controlled by Pakistan.

LTTE: Liberation Tigers of Tamil Eelam.

Mercosur: Mercado Común del Sur. A free trade agreement between Argentina, Brazil, Paraguay and Uruguay.

NAFTA: North American Free Trade Agreement.

NGOs: Non-Govermental Organisations.

Pakhtoons: Tribal inhabitants of the North West Frontier Provinces and surrounding areas. Also known as Pathans.

Pro-Azadi: Factions supporting the freedom of Kashmir ('Azad Kashmir').

SAARC: South Asian Association for Regional Cooperation.

SAPA: South Asian Preferential Trading Agreement.

SADC: South African Development Community.

Simla Agreement: An agreement facilitating the resumption of trade and cooperation in economic and other agreed fields signed by India's Prime Minister Indira Gandhi and Pakistani President Zulfikar Ali Bhutto on 2 July 1972.

Taliban: A fundamentalist Islamic militia. In 1995 the Taliban militia took over Afghanistan and in 1996 took Kabul and set up an Islamic government.

Tashkent Agreement: Signed on 10 January 1966 in the aftermath of the 1965 war, the Soviet-brokered agreement required that India and Pakistan withdraw their troops by 26 February 1966, to positions held prior to 5 August 1965, and observe the ceasefire line agreed to on 30 June 1965.

Ulema: The body of mullahs (Muslim scholars trained in Islam and Islamic law) who are the interpreters of Islam's sciences, doctrines and laws. They are the chief guarantors of continuity in the spiritual and intellectual history of the Islamic community.

Vinoba Bhave (1895-1982): Scholar, saint and often referred to as Mahatma Gandhi's 'spiritual successor,' Vinoba Bhave was posthumously honoured with the Bharat Ratna Award in 1984.

China ASEAN Free Trade Area: The treaty on ASEAN-China Comprehensive Economic Cooperation was signed between China and ASEAN leaders at the China-ASEAN Summit meeting in 2001. It set out to establish the China-ASEAN Free Trade Area by 2010, highlighting the great prospect of China's bilateral economic cooperation, mutual political trust, increased economic and trade exchanges.

Wilsonian: Relating to or suggestive of Woodrow Wilson. President Wilson's approach to international relations, especially his use of force, has become a model, which has influenced American foreign policy for almost eighty years. Many recent American operations have reflected Wilsonian ideas and ideals. Over the years, Wilson's model has proven to be quite resilient.

WMDs: Weapons of mass destruction.